THE ASCENT
OF THE WEST

FROM PREHISTORY
THROUGH THE
RENAISSANCE

A History of Western Civilization

THE ASCENT
OF THE WEST

FROM PREHISTORY
THROUGH THE
RENAISSANCE

EDITED BY HEATHER M. CAMPBELL, SENIOR EDITOR,
GEOGRAPHY AND HISTORY

Britannica®
Educational Publishing

IN ASSOCIATION WITH

ROSEN
EDUCATIONAL SERVICES

Educational Publishing
ritannica, Inc.)
tional Services, LLC
Y 10010.

Britannica, Inc. Britannica, Encyclopædia Britannica,
ed trademarks of Encyclopædia Britannica, Inc. All

Distributed exclusively by Rosen Educational Services.
For a listing of additional Britannica Educational Publishing titles, call toll free (800) 237-9932.

First Edition

Britannica Educational Publishing
Michael I. Levy: Executive Editor
J.E. Luebering: Senior Manager
Marilyn L. Barton: Senior Coordinator, Production Control
Steven Bosco: Director, Editorial Technologies
Lisa S. Braucher: Senior Producer and Data Editor
Yvette Charboneau: Senior Copy Editor
Kathy Nakamura: Manager, Media Acquisition
Heather M. Campbell: Senior Editor, Geography and History

Rosen Educational Services
Jeanne Nagle: Senior Editor
Shalini Saxena: Editor
Nelson Sá: Art Director
Cindy Reiman: Photography Manager
Matthew Cauli: Designer, Cover Design
Introduction by Laura Loria

Library of Congress Cataloging-in-Publication Data

The ascent of the West : from prehistory through the Renaissance / edited by Heather M. Campbell.—1st ed.
    p. cm.—(A history of Western civilization)
"In association with Britannica Educational Publishing, Rosen Educational Services."
Includes bibliographical references and index.
ISBN 978-1-61530-299-4 (library binding)
1. Civilization, Western—History. I. Campbell, Heather M.
CBS245.A77 2011
909.09821—dc22

2010014142

Manufactured in the United States of America

On the cover: *The Marriage of the Virgin* by High Renaissance artist Raffaello Sanzio, known simply as Raphael. *The Bridgeman Art Library/Getty Images*

On page x: Ruins at the Minoan city-state at Knossos, on the island of Crete. The Minoans heavily influenced the Mycenaean civilization, which was one of the earliest Indo-European cultures to inhabit Greece. *Travel Ink/Gallo Images/Getty Images*

On pages 1, 24, 68, 89, 162, 209, 211, 213: Prehistoric image of a horse decorating a cave in Lascaux, France. *Hulton Archive/Getty Images*

CONTENTS

Introduction

Chapter 1: Prehistory   1
  Paleolithic Settlement   1
    Earliest Developments   2
    Upper Paleolithic Developments   4
  Mesolithic Adaptations   8
    Hunting and Gathering Culture   9
  The Neolithic Period   13
    The Adoption of Farming   13
    LBK Culture   17
    The Late Neolithic Period   18
    The Indo-Europeans   22

Chapter 2: The Metal Ages   **24**
  The Chronology of the Metal Ages   25
    Urnfield Culture   27
  Characteristics of the Copper Age   27
  Characteristics of the Bronze Age   29
    Bell Beaker Culture   34
  Characteristics of the Iron Age   35
  Social and Economic Developments   36
    Control Over Resources   37
    Changing Centres of Wealth   41
    Prestige and Status   45
    The Relationship Between Nature
    and Culture   55
    Rituals, Religion, and Art   56
  The People of the Metal Ages   62

**Chapter 3: Greeks, Romans, and
Barbarians**   **68**
  Greeks   68
    A Nation of City-States   69
    People of Achievement   70
    Political Developments   72

Greek Influence 72
Achaean League 74
Romans 74
   The Roman Empire 75
   Roman Government and
   Citizenry 77
   The Empire's Decline 78
   Rome and Christianity 78
Barbarian Migrations and Invasions 80
   The Germans and Huns 81
   The Reconfiguration of
   the Empire 86

Chapter 4: The Middle Ages 89
The Idea of the Middle Ages 91
   The Term and Concept Before
   the 18th Century 92
   Enlightenment Scorn and
   Romantic Admiration 95
   The Middle Ages in Modern
   Historiography 97
   Chronology 100
Late Antiquity: The Reconfiguration
of the Roman World 101
   The Organization of Late
   Imperial Christianity 103
   Monasticism 107
   Kings and Peoples 108
   The Great Commission 109
   The Bishops of Rome 111
   Synod of Whitby 112
   The Mediterranean World
   Divided 114
The Frankish Ascendancy 115
   Charlemagne and the Carolingian
   Dynasty 115
   Merovingian Dynasty 116

Carolingian Decline and Its
Consequences   120
Growth and Innovation   122
    Demographic and Agricultural
    Growth   123
    Technological Innovations   126
    Urban Growth   127
Reform and Renewal   129
The Consequences of Reform   133
    The Transformation of Thought
    and Learning   133
    Ecclesiastical Organization   137
    Devotional Life   143
    The Emergence of a New
    Ecclesiastical Discipline   147
    Christianity, Judaism, and Islam   149
From Territorial Principalities to
Territorial Monarchies   152
    The Office and Person of
    the King   152
    Crusades   153
    Instruments of Royal
    Governance   155
    The Three Orders   156
Crisis, Recovery, and Resilience   159

Chapter 5: The Renaissance   **162**
The Italian Renaissance   163
    Urban Growth   164
    Wars of Expansion   168
    Italian Humanism   170
    Renaissance Thought   180
The Northern Renaissance   188
    Political, Economic, and Social
    Background   188
    Northern Humanism   195
    Christian Mystics   198

The Growth of Vernacular
    Literature   200
Renaissance Science and
    Technology   202
Conclusion   206

Glossary   209
Bibliography   211
Index   213

INTRODUCTION

The topic of European history often focuses on the great kingdoms and republics of modern Europe, along with the wars that consumed them. While those themes are important, they are most prominent only during the last 500 years. There also is a long period of prehistoric, ancient, and medieval development during which Europe was not neatly divided into countries and their individual cultures. In fact, the relative cultural homogeneity of prehistoric times evolved into greater diversity over thousands of years. This book examines the early history of Europe, leading up to its emergence as a continent of powerful nation-states that exerted influence around the globe.

Archaeological evidence discovered since the mid-19th century shows the first anatomically modern humans in Europe to have lived during the Paleolithic Period, also called the Old Stone Age (35,000–8300 BC). Prior to the appearance of modern humans, archaic humans called Neanderthals, colloquially known as cavemen, roamed the Continent. They survived mainly by hunting, sometimes scavenging meat from dead animals, and they used simple stone tools for chopping and cutting. By contrast, humans of the Old Stone Age made more sophisticated tools not only of stone, notably flint, but also of bone and antler. Migrating south and building more permanent homes, they hunted small game, buried their dead, and produced art in the forms of jewelry and representational figures. Similar art pieces are found throughout Europe, suggesting social grouping and alliances between groups, which undoubtedly aided their survival. People of the Mesolithic Period, which began about 8300 BC, invented trapping tools such as nets and hooks. A warmer climate also allowed humans of this time to benefit from an increase in available plant life for consumption.

During the Neolithic Period that followed, beginning between the 7th and 4th millennia BC, depending on
location, humans in Europe adopted agriculture. Those
in Greece were the earliest farmers; they cultivated flax,
wheat, and barley beginning about 7000 BC, while other
European areas did not see the introduction of agriculture for several millennia. From the late 4th millennium
BC, agricultural innovations included the keeping of animal herds to provide not only meat but also milk, wool,
and labour, as well as the implementation of irrigation
systems, as in Spain. Socially, burial evidence indicates a
greater prestige accorded to males and those with relative
material wealth. The most common languages belonged to
the Indo-European language group, which also stretched
to Central Asia and India. Possible explanations for these
related languages are invasions or migrations from the
East.

As the Neolithic Period drew to a close, societies in
Europe began producing metals. These developments
were independent of similar advances made in the Middle
East. The three European Metal Ages (3200–1 BC)—
Copper, Bronze, and Iron—brought with them significant
social change, according to the physical record of objects
left behind. Copper was important as a status symbol: the
chief use of copper appears to have been the adornment of
the dead, as in the Millaran culture of southeastern Spain.
Copper was not useful in tool making, but bronze, an alloy
of copper and tin or other metals, was more practical in
this regard. Bronze Age (2300–700 BC) development was
not uniform across Europe, and metal-producing societies were not necessarily more advanced than others.
Items made of bronze included daggers and the lur, a
hollow musical instrument made with the use of a mold.
Swords and armour first appeared during the Bronze Age.

Although the importance of war at this time is difficult to determine, an increase in fortified villages, such as Spišský Štvrtok, positioned on a trade route in Slovakia, indicate the development of intersocietal aggression and desire for economic control. Iron gradually came into favour over bronze and was preferred over stone and wood not only for tools and weapons but also in agricultural production. As iron production flourished and bronze faded in importance, the Continent's centres of wealth and paths of trade shifted.

The Metal Ages brought numerous social and economic changes. Evidence of hoarding in the Bronze Age suggests a religious significance behind the practice or an emphasis on conspicuous consumption, while the less common Iron Age hoards, consisting mainly of weapons, most likely were collected in preparation for war or taken as the spoils of war. The people of the Metal Ages increasingly saw themselves as members of tribes, though not necessarily of the same ethnicity. Grave placement and burial objects indicate the emergence of social stratification, as do human remains themselves. Studies of Iron Age bones have shown a marked difference in the wear on the bodies of those who laboured and those who were spared a life of toil.

Toward the end of the Metal Ages came the emergence of the first European civilizations—sophisticated cultures marked by the construction of cities, the use of writing, and the creation of complex political, social, and economic systems. The ancient Greeks and Romans were the central players in this historical advance, described as the Classical period of European history. Greece evolved as a collection of individual city-states that frequently aligned in leagues and, perhaps just as frequently, broke those alliances. The Greeks were the originators of European philosophy and science, and are also highly regarded for their art, architecture, and poetry. When Macedonia conquered Greece in the 4th century BC, the Greek language and culture spread though its vast domain.

Rome, which incorporated Greek thought into its own culture, rapidly colonized Europe, notably during the 2nd century AD, and spread its political structures, military institutions, laws, and language. The people of conquered territories were able to gain Roman citizenship and send men to the capital to fill high offices, and they largely adopted Roman culture as their own. The provinces traded freely and found markets for their products throughout the empire. Christianity, from the 4th century AD the sanctioned religion of the Roman Empire, became a strong guiding force in western Europe. However, after the split of the empire into two halves in 285, the west suffered from fewer resources than the east, which was centred on Constantinople (now Istanbul, Turkey). The western economy became more rural and localized; as trade diminished, so did the dissemination of Roman ideas. The western capital even was moved away from Rome, north to Ravenna (Italy).

As Rome thus weakened, migrating and invading Germanic peoples, known to the Romans as barbarians, clashed with Roman forces at the edges of the empire. Various Germanic tribes became increasingly powerful as they won important battles, were enriched by the spoils of war, and even infiltrated the Roman army. Barbarians ultimately toppled the western portion of the Roman Empire in the 5th century AD. (The eastern half continued on as the Byzantine Empire.)

As the Byzantine and, farther east, Islamic civilizations developed distinct identities, Europe—the heir of the Western Roman Empire—also became a cultural entity during the Middle Ages (c. 500–1500). The structure of the

Christian church was the greatest influence on Europe's development during this time. In the 5th and 6th centuries, bishops replaced local government as administrators and suppliers of goods to cities; they ultimately became the most powerful church leaders during the first half of the Middle Ages. Priests served the people on a day-to-day basis, and monks devoted their lives to work, prayer, and contemplation. The church called itself Catholic to reflect the universality of the practice of Christianity. More and more cultures became Christian through collective conversion under their rulers. Throughout Europe, the local rulers, or kings, of various peoples, viewed themselves as God's servants.

The strong, independent monarchy of the Franks (5th–9th centuries) upheld Christianity's supremacy and brought much of western Europe under Frankish control. The kings of the Carolingian dynasty of Franks believed they were restoring the unity of the western European world. The greatest Carolingian king, Charlemagne, expanded Frankish dominance beyond the borders of the old Western Roman Empire and became known as "the father of Europe." He encouraged the work of monks and their production of written works, set high standards of education and morality for clergy, and spread uniform canon laws in the 8th and 9th centuries. In AD 800 he persuaded the bishop of Rome, Leo III, to crown him emperor of the Romans, a prestigious title that preceded that of Holy Roman emperor—the lay ruler of the large collection of European lands known from the 12th century as the Holy Roman Empire.

After the Carolingian line died out, so did the ascendancy of kings. Society was divided into three groups: those who prayed, those who fought, and those who laboured. The warriors, or lords, controlled the land, which was worked by peasants who were subject to their rule. Agricultural growth over the next few centuries led to a population explosion, but peasant status dropped lower, to serfdom. Technological advances of this time included water mills and windmills, horse stirrups and collars, and the imposing, architecturally complex Gothic cathedrals. Cities functioned as centres for cathedrals and commerce, which encouraged nonfood production. Guilds were formed to standardize crafts and to protect artisans, and trade with other cities grew. Urban dwellers gained a reputation for possessing proper Christian belief and sophisticated manners, while rural people were thought of as backward.

The Gregorian Reform of the church in the 11th century established stricter codes for clergy, including the requirement of celibacy, and articulated the authority of the bishop of Rome—the pope—over both clergy and laity. The declaration of papal authority resulted in a lasting conflict between the papacy and the Holy Roman emperors. As the office of emperor lost much of its religious character, it retained only a theoretical ascendancy over other secular rulers. In reality, individual kings, formerly the local leaders of groups of people, gradually became recognized also as the rulers of the lands those people inhabited. To assist them in their reign, monarchs appointed various councils and assemblies, such as Parliament in England. They appeased the nobility with land and titles, increasing their loyalty to the monarch, thus increasing his personal power.

The Middle Ages culminated in a series of disasters. The 14th century was marked by famine, plague, and invasions by Mongols. Nevertheless, the European population recovered, thanks to the stability of the social and economic systems in place. Italy especially flourished, despite a massive banking failure. The city-states of Florence, Milan, and Venice continually fought for dominance, and while doing so introduced balance-of-power diplomacy.

Meanwhile, an Italian revival of the Classical ideals of Greece and Rome, a movement termed Italian humanism, emphasized the growth of literacy, a shift from religious to secular concerns, and study of the liberal arts: rhetoric, grammar, poetry, moral philosophy, history, music, and mathematics. Originally, humanists preferred the languages of the ancients, Greek and Latin, but eventually works in Italian were considered acceptable. Indeed, great literature was perhaps the chief achievement of the Italian Renaissance, which gave to Europe the works of Dante and Niccolò Machiavelli.

Northern Europe also had a period of artistic and intellectual achievement at the end of the Middle Ages. However, the Northern Renaissance had a Christian spirit, unlike that of Italy, where the secular ideals of courtly manners and linguistic skill were emphasized. During this time Christian mystics devoted their lives to contemplation and a direct connection with their spirituality. Literature in one's native tongue gained recognition in northern Europe as well. Geoffrey Chaucer's *The Canterbury Tales* and the works of William Shakespeare are some of the best-known examples.

The Renaissance also saw new scientific thought, including the rejection of an Earth-centred universe by Nicolaus Copernicus. Artists such as Leonardo da Vinci emphasized the mathematical order of the natural world. These ideas were able to spread throughout Europe chiefly through the invention of the printing press in 15th-century Germany. Information traveled across the Continent faster than it ever had, to an increasingly literate population.

Politically, by the end of the 15th century France and Spain had established firm boundaries and relative stability, and kingship was the dominant form of leadership in most places. Economically, the feudal system declined as manufacturing increased, and cities became known for their specialized markets, such as London's cloth and banking industries, or Sevilla's location as the gateway to the Americas.

Europe began as a scattering of people concerned only with their own survival. Emerging social order gave stability to groups of individuals. Trade fostered the sharing of ideas, and technology improved the standard of living over time. Political ambition and leadership created strong kingdoms capable of providing infrastructure for a growing population. The relative stability of medieval Europe allowed the flourishing of art, science, and philosophy. By the end of the Middle Ages, Europe had transformed itself into a culturally cohesive, if not truly unified, civilization.

PREHISTORY

The appearance of anatomically modern humans in Europe about 35,000 BC was accompanied by major changes in culture and technology. There was a further period of significant change after the last major Pleistocene glaciation (the Pleistocene Epoch occurred from about 2.6 million to 11,700 years ago), which included the widespread adoption of farming and the establishment of permanent settlements from the 7th millennium BC. These laid the foundation for all future developments of European civilization.

Knowledge of these early periods of the European past is entirely dependent on archaeology. The evidence, which has almost all been collected since the middle of the 19th century, varies greatly from region to region and is limited by what was deposited and by whether what was deposited has survived. The archaeological evidence has also been disturbed by a range of human and natural processes, from glacial activity to farming and modern development. Modern techniques have greatly increased the amount of information available, but many parts of the story of the past may be difficult or impossible to recover, and the evidence that has been revealed needs to be assessed in the light of all these factors.

PALEOLITHIC SETTLEMENT

The period of human activity to the end of the last major Pleistocene glaciation, about 8300 BC, is termed the Paleolithic Period (Old Stone Age). That part of it from 35,000 to 8300 BC is termed the Upper Paleolithic.

The climatic record shows a cyclic pattern of warmer and colder periods; in the last 750,000 years, there have been eight major cycles, with many shorter episodes. In the colder periods, the Arctic and Alpine ice sheets expanded, and sea levels fell. Some parts of southern Europe may have been little affected by these changes, but the advance and retreat of the ice sheets and accompanying glacial environments had a significant impact on northern Europe; at their maximum advance, they covered most of Scandinavia, the North European Plain, and Russia. Human occupation fluctuated in response to these changing conditions, but continuous settlement north of the Alps required a solution to the problems of living in extremely cold conditions.

EARLIEST DEVELOPMENTS

By one million years ago hominins were widely distributed in Africa and Asia, and some finds in Europe may be that early as well. The earliest securely dated material is from Isernia la Pineta in southern Italy, where stone tools and animal bones were dated to about 730,000 BC. Thereafter the evidence becomes more plentiful, and by 375,000 BC most areas except Scandinavia, the Alps, and northern Eurasia had been colonized.

Fossil remains of the hominins themselves are rare, and most of the evidence consists of stone tools. The simplest were chopping tools made from pebbles with a few flakes struck off to create an edge. These were replaced by more complex traditions of toolmaking, which produced a range of hand axes and flake tools; these industries are referred to as Acheulean, after the French site of Saint-Acheul. Some of the tools were for woodworking, but only rarely do any tools of organic material, such as wooden spears, survive as evidence of other Paleolithic technologies.

Stone blades discovered at Saint-Acheul, France. Tools and fossilized biotic remains give archaeologists insight into prehistoric European civilizations. The Bridgeman Art Library/Getty Images

The subsistence economy depended on hunting and gathering. Population densities were necessarily low, and group territories were large. The main evidence is animal bones, which suggest a varied reliance on species such as rhinoceros, red deer, ibex, and horse, but it is difficult to reconstruct how such food was actually acquired. Open confrontation with large animals, such as the rhinoceros, is unlikely, and they were probably killed in vulnerable locations such as lake-edge watering spots. At La Cotte de Sainte Brelade in the Channel Islands, rhinoceroses and mammoths were driven over a cliff edge. Scavenging meat from already dead animals also may have been important. Food resources such as migratory herds and plants were available only seasonally, so an annual strategy for survival was necessary. While carcasses of dead animals frozen in the snow would have provided a store of food, it is not always clear how it was possible to store food acquired at times of plenty.

From the beginning of the last major Pleistocene glaciation about 120,000 BC, the hominin fossils belong to the Neanderthals, who have been found throughout Europe and western Asia, including the glacial environments of central Europe. They were biologically and culturally adapted to survival in the harsh environments of the north, though they are also found in more moderate climates in southern Europe and Asia. Finds of stone tools from the Russian plains suggest the first certain evidence of colonization there by 80,000 BC. Despite their heavy skeletons and developed brow ridges, Neanderthals were probably little different from modern humans. Some of the skeletal remains appear to be from deliberate burials, the first evidence for such advanced behaviour among humans.

UPPER PALEOLITHIC DEVELOPMENTS

From about 35,000 BC, anatomically modern humans—*Homo sapiens sapiens*, the ancestor of modern populations—were found throughout Europe, and the following period was marked by a series of important technological and cultural changes, in marked contrast to the comparative stability of the preceding hundreds of thousands of years. These changes cannot be simply explained as the result of the sudden appearance of modern, intelligent humans. The preceding Neanderthals differed little in brain size, and some Neanderthal remains are associated with tool assemblages of the new technology as well as with behavioral practices such as burial. The problem of the relationship of the Neanderthals to the sudden appearance of modern humans is difficult; possible explanations include total replacement of Neanderthals by modern populations, interbreeding with an immigrant modern population, or Neanderthals as ancestors of modern humans.

The technological changes of the Upper Paleolithic Period include the disappearance of heavy tools such as hand axes and choppers and the introduction of a much wider range of tools for special purposes, many of them made from long, thin blades. Tools made of antler, bone, and ivory were also widely used, apparently for the first time. After 18,000 BC there were further innovations. Flint was pretreated by heating to alter its structure and make flaking easier, and new tool types included harpoons, needles for sewing fur garments, and small blades for hafting in spears and arrows. The new technologies and more complex and specialized tool types suggest a major change in the pattern of energy expenditure. Much more effort was devoted to the careful use of resources, and tools were prepared in advance and retained, rather than made and discarded expediently.

Sites of this period are found throughout Europe, though at the height of the last major Pleistocene glaciation (about 35,000 to 13,000 BC) much of the North European Plain was abandoned as populations moved south. There is a greatly increased number of sites, many of which show evidence of more permanent structures such as hearths, pavements, and shelters built of skins on a frame of bone or wood. Some of this increase may be due to the greater likelihood of finding sites of this more recent period, but it may also indicate a growing population density and a greater investment of energy in construction.

Subsistence still depended on hunting and gathering, but the role of plant foods is difficult to estimate. As population increased, group territories may have become smaller, and the increasingly harsh environments of the last glaciation necessitated appropriate strategies for survival. Some sites show a concentration on particular large animal species (horse and reindeer in the north and ibex and red deer in the south), but there is also evidence for the increasing use of other food resources, such as rabbits, fish, and shellfish. In comparison with large animals, these produced small amounts of food, but they were an important addition because of their greater reliability. Settlement patterns reflect these social and economic strategies, which allowed most of the population to stay at one location for long periods while others left to procure distant resources.

Some of the most important evidence is for change in social organization and human behaviour. There is increasing evidence for deliberate and careful burial, sometimes with elaborate treatment of the dead. At Sungir in Russia and at Grotta Paglicci in Italy, for instance, the dead were buried with tools and ornaments, indicating a respect for their identity or status. Personal ornaments, especially bracelets, beads, and pendants, are common finds. They were made from a wide variety of materials, including animal teeth, ivory, and shells; some appear to have been sewn onto garments. Such ornamentation not only shows an elaboration of clothing and an interest in display but may also have been used as a means of signaling individual or group identity.

The earliest art objects in Europe also date from this period. There are small figurines of animals and humans made from finely carved bone or ivory. Among the most striking are the so-called Venus figurines, stylized representations of females with large breasts and buttocks, which show a marked degree of similarity from France to Russia. There are also thousands of small stone plaques engraved with representations of humans and animals.

Art is also found in caves, particularly in France and Spain, in caves such as Lascaux and Altamira, though there is one cave at Kapova in the Urals with decoration in a similar style. In some cases, reliefs of humans or animals are

6

Wall paintings from a section of a cave in Lascaux, France, known as the Hall of the Bulls. Lascaux Cave is filled with many examples of Upper Paleolithic artwork. Pierre Andrieu/AFP/Getty Images

carved on rock walls, but the most spectacular artworks are the paintings, dominated by large animals such as mammoth, horse, or bison; human figures are rare, but there are many other signs and symbols. The precise meaning of this art is impossible to recover, but it appears to have played a significant part in group ceremonial activity. Much of it is in almost inaccessible depths of caves and may have been important for rituals of hunting or initiation.

The similarity in style over great distances—seen most clearly in the case of the Venus figurines—is evidence for the existence of extensive social networks throughout Europe. Material items also were transmitted over long distances, especially particular types of flint, fossil shell, and marine mollusks. Such networks were most extensive at the height of the last glaciation and were an important social solution to the problem of surviving in extreme climates. They provided alliances to supply food and other material resources as well as information about a far-flung environment. Human developments during this so-called Ice Age thus included not only technological, economic, and social solutions to the problems of adaptation and survival but also an increased awareness of individual and group identity and a new field of symbolic and artistic activity.

MESOLITHIC ADAPTATIONS

The extreme conditions of the last Pleistocene glaciation began to improve about 13,000 BC as temperatures slowly rose. The Scandinavian Ice Sheet itself started to retreat northward about 8300 BC, and the period between then and the origins of agriculture (at various times in the 7th to 4th millennia, depending on location) was one of great environmental and cultural change. It is termed

Hunting and Gathering Culture

A hunting and gathering culture, also called a foraging culture, is any group of people that depends primarily on wild foods for subsistence. Until about 12,000 to 11,000 years ago, when agriculture and animal domestication emerged in southwest Asia and in Mesoamerica, all peoples were hunters and gatherers. Their strategies have been very diverse, depending greatly upon the local environment; foraging strategies have included hunting or trapping big game, hunting or trapping smaller animals, fishing, gathering shellfish or insects, and gathering wild plant foods such as fruits, vegetables, tubers, seeds, and nuts. Most hunters and gatherers combine a variety of these strategies in order to ensure a balanced diet.

A foraging economy usually demands an extensive land area. It has been estimated that people who depend on such methods must have available 7 to 500 square miles (18 to 1,300 square km) of land per capita, depending upon local environmental conditions. Permanent villages or towns are generally possible only where food supplies are unusually abundant and reliable.

Conditions of such abundance are rare, and most foraging groups must move whenever the local supply of food begins to be exhausted. In these cases possessions are limited to what can be carried from one camp to another. As housing must also be transported or made on the spot, it is usually simple, comprising huts, tents, or lean-tos made of plant materials or the skins of animals. Social groups are necessarily small because only a limited number of people can congregate together without quickly exhausting the food resources of a locality. Such groups typically comprise either extended family units or a number of related families collected together in a band. An individual band is generally small in number, typically with no more than 30 individuals if moving on foot, or perhaps 100 in a group with horses or other means of transport. However, each band is known across a wide area because all residents of a given region are typically tied to one another through a large network of kinship and reciprocity that will often congregate for a short period each year.

9

the Mesolithic Period (Middle Stone Age) to empha-
size its transitional importance, but the alternative term
Epipaleolithic, used mostly in eastern Europe, stresses the
continuity with processes begun earlier.

As the ice sheets retreated, vast areas of new land in
northern Europe were opened up for human occupation.
Resettlement began in some short warmer episodes at the
end of the last glaciation. In the longer term, the melting
of the Arctic glaciers produced a rise in sea levels, though
this was to some extent offset by a rise in land levels as the
weight of the overlying ice was removed. The combined
effect of these processes was to flood large areas of land in
the Mediterranean and especially in the North Sea Basin.
Britain was isolated from the continent during the 7th
millennium, and the modern coastline was broadly established by the 4th.

The changes in physical landforms were accompanied
by similarly major changes in the environment. The rising
temperature and humidity led to the increased growth of
plant life, including birch and pine as well as smaller trees
and bushes that produced nuts and fruit. Continued climatic amelioration meant further environmental change,
and the initial open forest progressively gave way to climax forest dominated by oak and elm, which crowded out
many of the smaller species. There were similar changes
among animals. The large animals of the Ice Age such as
bison and mammoth disappeared, either because of climatic change or from overhunting, and reindeer herds
moved northward in search of colder conditions. The
European forests were dominated by smaller animals,
such as wild cattle, pigs, and deer, with ibex in the south.

The evidence for human exploitation of these changing environments varies considerably, depending on the
precise range of regionally available resources. As the
reindeer moved north, so did some human groups. Others

Reindeer in Russia's Ural Mountains. Experts believe that some early European societies followed herds of these and other food-source animals northward, broadening population borders throughout the continent. Shutterstock.com

adapted to the new animal and plant resources available. Wild cattle, deer, and pigs were widely hunted, as well as many types of bird. Fish were also caught, including river species such as salmon and carp and many sea species. On the western coasts, shellfish also were exploited. The role of plant foods is difficult to estimate, but there is evidence for the use of many species, including hazelnuts and various berries.

These new patterns of economy needed new technologies. Stone tools increasingly took the form of small blades for tipping or hafting in arrows and spears. Where conditions allow their survival, it is possible to see many new tools and equipment made of organic materials, though some, such as the bow and arrow, may have been made in earlier periods. Hooks, nets, and traps for fishing; birch bark containers; and textiles made from plant fibres are all known. Canoes and paddles also have been found.

Though subsistence was dependent on hunting and gathering seasonally available resources, those resources could be managed in elementary ways. Hunting strategies concentrated on taking adult males, preserving the young and female animals needed to maintain the herds. Dogs were a source of meat and fur, but they may also have been used in hunting. It may have been possible to control the movement of herds by making clearances in the forest, thus attracting animals to the new growth; the evidence for fire and repeated small-scale clearances supports this theory. Plants may have been husbanded. In these ways, human control was exercised over the environment and its resources.

Human occupation expanded throughout Europe, and many areas show a pattern of settlement with base camps occupied by all members of the group for some part of the year and small sites used for the exploitation of some particular resource. Wide social networks continued to exist, as shown by the long-distance exchange of some raw materials such as special types of rock. Mobility may have been important for ensuring an adequate annual subsistence, but some environments, such as the coastal regions of the Baltic and the west, may have allowed the possibility of more permanent settlement. Reliance on fish and shellfish there might be thought a last resort. Alternatively, it could have been a purposive choice of resources that would allow permanent residence. Denmark and western France have traditions of deliberate human burial that support this theory.

Thus the environmental changes were met with a variety of social, economic, and technological responses, but human society did not adapt passively. Opportunities existed to manage the environment more actively and to make choices for social rather than purely survival purposes.

THE NEOLITHIC PERIOD

From about 7000 BC in Greece, farming economies were progressively adopted in Europe, though areas farther west, such as Britain, were not affected for two millennia and Scandinavia not until even later. The period from the beginning of agriculture to the widespread use of bronze about 2300 BC is called the Neolithic (New Stone Age).

THE ADOPTION OF FARMING

Agriculture had developed at an earlier date in the Middle East, and the relationship of Europe to that area and the mechanism of the introduction of agriculture have been variously explained. At one extreme is a model of immigrant colonization from the Middle East, with the agricultural frontier pushing farther westward as population grew and new settlements were founded. A variation of this model denies the uniformity of such a "wave of advance" and stresses the possibility of a more irregular pioneering movement. At the other extreme is a model of agricultural adoption by indigenous Mesolithic groups, with a minimum of reliance on any introduced people or resources.

In favour of the intrusive model is the nature of the crops that formed the basis of early agriculture; the main cereals were emmer wheat, einkorn wheat, and barley, together with other plants such as peas and flax. These had all been domesticated in the Middle East, where their wild progenitors were found. The material culture of the earliest farmers in Greece and southeastern Europe also shows great similarity to that of the Middle East. On the other hand, the animals important to early agriculture are not so clearly introduced. Wild sheep and goats may have been available in southern Europe, and cattle were probably domesticated in southeastern Europe at least as early as in the Middle East. There also were definite European contributions; the dog was domesticated in Europe in the Mesolithic Period, and evidence suggests that the horse was first domesticated on the Western Steppe.

The process of agricultural adoption, furthermore, was neither fast nor uniform. It took at least 4,000 years for farming to reach its northern limit in Scandinavia, and there it was the success of fishing and sealing that allowed agriculture as a desirable addition to the economy. In many areas of western Europe, it is likely that domesticated animals were used before the adoption of agricultural plants. It is also possible to argue for a considerable Mesolithic contribution, especially in the north and west. Not only did some areas continue to rely on hunting and gathering in addition to farming but there was also continuity of settlement location and resource use, especially of stone for tools. Despite the disappearance of the small blades previously used for spears and arrows and the appearance of heavy tools for forest clearance, there was some continuity of tool technology.

The adoption of farming is unlikely to have been a simple or uniform process throughout Europe. In some regions, especially Greece, the Balkans, southern Italy, central Europe, and Ukraine, actual colonization by new populations may have been important. Elsewhere, especially in the west and north, a gradual process of adaptation by indigenous communities is more likely, though everywhere the pattern would have been mixed.

The consequences of the adoption of farming were important for all later developments. Permanent settlement, population growth, and exploitation of smaller territories all brought about new relationships between people and the environment. Mobility had previously necessitated small populations at low densities and had allowed only material items that could be carried, with little investment in structures; these restraints were removed, and the opportunity was created for many new crafts and technologies.

The earliest evidence for agriculture comes from sites in Greece, such as Knossos and Argissa, soon after 7000 BC. During the 7th millennium, farming was widespread in southeastern Europe. The material culture of this region bears a strong similarity to that of the Middle East. Pottery making was introduced, and a variety of highly decorated vessels was produced. Permanent settlements of small mud-brick houses were established, and continuous rebuilding of such villages on the same spot produced large settlement mounds, or tells. Clay figurines, mostly female, are common finds in many houses, and there may also have been special shrines or temples. The precise beliefs cannot be ascertained, but they suggest the importance of ritual and religion in these societies. By the 5th and 4th millennia, some of these sites, such as Sesklo and Dhimini in Greece, were defended. From the early 5th millennium, there is evidence for the development of copper and gold metallurgy, independently of Middle Eastern traditions, and copper mines have been found in the Balkan Peninsula. Metal products included personal ornaments as well as some functional items; the cemetery at Varna, Bulg., contained many gold objects, with large collections in some graves. Control of ritual, technology, and agriculture, as well as the need for defense, all suggest the growing differentiation within Neolithic society.

In the central and western Mediterranean, the clearest evidence is from southern Italy, where a mixed farming economy was established in the 7th millennium. Many large villages, often surrounded by enclosure ditches, have been recognized. Elsewhere in the region, domesticated crops and animals were adopted more slowly into the indigenous economies. New technologies also were adopted;

pottery decorated with characteristic impressed patterns
was made, and by the 4th millennium copper was being
worked in Spain. The major islands of the Mediterranean
were colonized. The general picture is one of small-scale
regional development. One such regional pattern was on
Malta, where a series of massive stone temples was constructed from the early 4th millennium.

In a band across central and western Europe, the earliest farmers from 5400 BC onward are represented by a
homogeneous pattern of settlements and material culture, named the LBK culture (from *Linienbandkeramik* or
Linearbandkeramik), after the typical pottery decorated
with linear bands of ornament. The same styles of pottery
and other material are found throughout the region, and
their settlements show a regular preference for the easily
worked and well-drained loess soils. The houses were 20
to 23 feet (6 to 7 metres) wide and up to 150 feet (45.72
metres) long and possibly included stalling for animals. In
some areas they were grouped in large villages, but elsewhere there was a dispersed pattern of small clusters of
houses. Some known cemeteries show a concentration of
objects deposited with older males. About 4700 BC the
cultural homogeneity ended, and regional patterns of settlement and culture appeared as the population grew and
new areas were exploited for farming. Some of the best
information comes from villages on the edges of lakes in
France and Switzerland, where organic material has been
preserved in damp conditions.

Farming also spread northeastward into the steppe
north of the Black Sea. Before 6000 BC domesticated
animals and pottery were found there, but in societies
that still relied heavily on hunting and fishing. By about
4500 BC a new pattern of villages, such as at Cucuteni
and Tripolye, was established with a mixed farming economy. Some of these villages contained many hundreds of

LBK Culture

The Neolithic LBK culture expanded over large areas of Europe north and west of the Danube River (from Slovakia to the Netherlands) about the 5th millennium BC. Farmers probably practiced a form of shifting cultivation on the loess soil. Emmer wheat and barley were grown, and domestic animals, usually cattle, were kept. The most common stone tool was a polished stone adze. The people occupied large rectangular houses grouped in medium-sized village communities or as small, dispersed clusters.

houses in a planned layout, and they were increasingly surrounded by massive fortifications. Farther east across the steppe as far as the southern Urals, pottery, domesticated animals, and cereals were progressively added to an indigenous hunting and gathering economy, and the horse was domesticated. Nomadic pastoral economies developed by the 2nd millennium.

Farming extended from central to northern Europe only after a long interval. For a millennium, agriculturalists and hunter-gatherers were in contact and pottery was adopted or exchanged, but domesticated animals and crops were only introduced into northern Germany, Poland, and southern Scandinavia about 4200 BC, apparently after a decline in the availability of marine food resources. Farming was rapidly adopted as the mainstay of subsistence and expanded to its maximum climatic viability in Scandinavia. By the middle of the 4th millennium, large communal tombs were being built, frequently of megalithic (large-stone) construction.

In western Europe, there was a similar delay in the spread of farming. In western France, domesticated animals were added to hunting and gathering in a predominantly stock-based economy, and pottery was also adopted. In Britain and Ireland, forest clearance as early as 4700 BC may represent the beginnings of agriculture, but there is little evidence for settlements or monuments before 4000 BC, and hunting and gathering economies survived in places. The construction of large communal tombs and defended enclosures from 4000 BC may mark the growth of agricultural populations and the beginning of competition for resources. Some of the enclosures were attacked and burned, clear evidence of violent warfare. The tombs, of earth and timber or of megalithic construction, contained communal burials and served as markers for claims to farming territories as well as foci for the worship of ancestors. Some, such as the tombs of Brittany and Ireland, contained elaborately decorated stones.

THE LATE NEOLITHIC PERIOD

From the late 4th millennium a number of developments in the agricultural economy became prominent. They did not, however, begin all at once nor were they found everywhere. Some of them may have been in use for some time, and there also are distinct regional variations. Cumulatively, however, they add up to a new phase of agricultural organization.

AGRICULTURAL INTENSIFICATION

One of the most important developments was the management of animal herds for purposes other than the provision of meat. In the case of cattle, there is some evidence for milk production earlier, but dairying appears to have taken on a much more significant role from this time. Oxen were raised to provide traction, and sheep were managed not for meat but primarily as a source of manure and wool. Textiles in the early Neolithic Period were predominantly made of flax, but from the early 3rd millennium wool was widely used, and spinning and weaving became important crafts and new ways of exploiting agricultural resources. New crops also were introduced. The most important were the vine and the olive, found in Greece from the early 3rd millennium. These tree crops represented an important addition to the range of agricultural produce and formed the basis for later developments in the Aegean.

There were also new technologies, especially the use of animal traction for the plow and for wheeled vehicles. The earliest evidence for plowing consists of marks preserved in the soil under burial mounds and dated to the end of the 4th millennium. A clay model of a wheeled cart of the same date is known from a grave at Szigetszentmárton, Hung., and actual wheels from northern Europe by 2500 BC. In southeastern Spain, the most arid area of Europe, irrigation systems were probably introduced. These all represent

Clay model of a wheeled cart, from a grave at Szigetszentmárton, Hung., end of the 4th millennium BC; in the Hungarian National Museum, Budapest. © Hungarian National Museum, Budapest; photograph, Kardos Judit

important new technologies applied to agriculture and an intensification of energy expenditure in that field.

The innovations outlined above marked the development of early agriculture toward a system more specifically adapted to the European environment and capable of producing a much wider range of outputs, especially of nonfood products. Some, such as wine and cloth, had a particular social significance, and others, especially the wheeled vehicle, led to further developments. The new agricultural regime also showed a better adaptation to the wide variety of regional environments in Europe and permitted expansion into new ecological zones. Whereas the earliest farmers mostly preferred the prime arable soils, such as the loess of central Europe, it was now possible, especially with the use of sheep, to exploit many less fertile soils.

SOCIAL CHANGE

The period from the late 4th millennium also saw many important social changes. They varied from region to region but laid the foundations for the society of the Bronze Age, which followed.

In southeastern Europe about 3200 BC, there was a major break in material culture and settlement patterns. The old styles of decorated pottery were replaced with new plainer forms, and the evidence for ritual, such as the figurines, ends. Many of the long-occupied tell sites were abandoned; the new settlement pattern shows many smaller sites and some larger ones which may have played a central role. In Greece there were similar changes, with population expansion especially in the south and the emergence of some sites as centres of authority; this period marked the beginning of the Aegean Bronze Age.

Elsewhere in the Mediterranean the changes are most marked in parts of Iberia. At Los Millares in southeastern

Spain and in southern Portugal at sites such as Vila Nova de São Pedro, strongly fortified settlements accompanied by cemeteries containing rich collections of prestige goods suggest the appearance of a more hierarchically organized society. Similar trends toward the emergence of sites of central authority took place in southern France, but there is little sign of such developments in Italy.

In central and northern Europe, changes of a different nature began about 2800 BC. The most obvious feature is two phases of new burial rites, comprising individual rather than communal burials with a particular emphasis on the deposition of prestige grave goods with adult males. The first phase, characterized by Corded Ware pottery and stone battle-axes, is found particularly in central and northern Europe. The second phase, dated to 2500–2200 BC, is marked by Bell Beaker pottery and the frequent occurrence of copper daggers in the graves; it is

Figurines believed to be female idols unearthed from the Los Millares site in Spain. Idols carved from imported materials were generally owned by the wealthier members of prehistoric European societies. G. Nimatallah/De Agostini Picture Library/Getty Images

found from Hungary to Britain and as far south as Italy, Spain, and North Africa. At the same time, there was an increase in the exchange of prestige goods such as amber, copper, and tools from particular rock sources.

Both of these burial rites have been attributed to invading population groups. On the other hand, they may also be seen as a new expression of an ideology of social status, emphasizing control of resources rather than ancestral descent. Such an explanation fits better with a picture of slow internal development within European society. The new ideology did not prevail everywhere, however, and in Britain, for instance, the 3rd millennium saw the construction of massive ceremonial monuments such as Avebury and Stonehenge, before the introduction of individual burial rites at the end of the millennium.

THE INDO-EUROPEANS

When there is evidence for the languages spoken in Europe at the end of the prehistoric period, it is clear that with few exceptions, such as Basque or Etruscan, they belonged to the Indo-European language group, which also extended to India and Central Asia. This raises the question of when these languages, or their ancestral prototype, were first spoken in Europe. One theory links these languages with a particular population of Indo-Europeans and explains the expansion of the languages as the result of invasion or immigration; their origin is sought in the east, perhaps in the area north of the Black and Caspian seas. The invasion is associated with the new patterns of settlement, economy, material culture, burial, and social organization seen about 3000 BC. These innovations, however, may be better attributed to internal developments. An alternative explanation for the origin of Indo-European languages associates it with the immigration of the first farmers from Anatolia at the beginning of the Neolithic Period, but the spread of farming does not seem to have been a uniform process or to have been achieved everywhere by population migration. There is, however, no single archaeological pattern that might correspond to a migration on an appropriate geographic scale throughout Europe, and all these explanations raise fundamental questions about the development, spread, and adoption of languages, the relationship of language to ethnic groups, and the correspondence of archaeologically recognizable patterns of material culture to either language or ethnicity.

CHAPTER 2

THE METAL AGES

The period of the 3rd, the 2nd, and the 1st millennia BC was a time of drastic change in Europe. This has traditionally been defined as the Metal Ages, which may be further divided into stages, with these approximate dates: the Bronze Age (2300–700 BC) and the Iron Age (700–1 BC), both of which followed a less distinctly defined Copper Age (c. 3200–2300 BC). At this time, societies in Europe began consciously to produce metals. Simultaneous with these technological innovations were changes in settlement organization, ritual life, and the interaction between the different societies in Europe. These developments and their remarkable reflections in the material culture make the period appear as a series of dramatic changes.

Local developments were long thought to have been caused by influences from the eastern Mediterranean and the Middle East and by migrations. Thus it was suggested that the segmented faience beads from the rich early Bronze Age graves in Wessex were actually Mycenaean products, or that development of bronze working in central Europe was due to the Aegean civilization's need for new bronze supplies. New methods of absolute dating, including radiocarbon dating, revolutionized the understanding of this phase in prehistoric Europe. They showed that many supposedly interdependent developments had in fact developed independently and had been separated by centuries. The Metal Ages of Europe thus must be understood as indigenous local inventions and as an independent cultural evolution. There were influences from, and contact with, the Middle East, and there were some migrations of people, especially from the Russian steppes; but the Metal

Ages in Europe were in general far more locally independent phenomena than had been recognized. They grew
out of conditions created in the Neolithic Period and the
Copper Age, followed their own trajectory in Europe, and
resulted in a range of new expressions in material culture
and in new social concerns.

THE CHRONOLOGY OF THE METAL AGES

Changes in metal objects, in styles, and in burial rituals
have been used to subdivide the period. The most basic
division uses the same criteria as Christian Jürgensen
Thomsen's Three Age system, in which the material used
for producing tools and weapons distinguishes an age. This
has resulted in a distinction between the Copper, Bronze,
and Iron ages, each of which has been further divided. In
temperate Europe all these subdivisions consist of relative
chronologies, and in such systems synchronizations and
comparisons among regions are vital. For the Bronze Age,
synchronization is possible, since this was a period of long-
distance contacts and trade between different regions. The
period had in many ways a remarkable coherence, and it
has been likened to the Common Market of the European
Union. On this basis a general chronological framework
has been developed that, using the changes in burial rites
and metal assemblages, divides the Bronze Age into either
Early, Middle, and Late phases or into the Unetician,
Tumulus, and Urnfield cultures. Synchronizations of the
more detailed local subdivisions, which were based on
typology of metal objects and cross-associations, have
employed schemes of Paul Reinecke and Oscar Montelius.
Oscar Montelius' chronology was developed on the basis
of Scandinavian bronze objects and resulted in a division of
the Bronze Age into Montelius I–VI, while Paul Reinecke

used south German material to divide it into shorter time sequences known as Bronze Age A–D and Hallstatt (Ha) A–D, with Hallstatt C marking the transition to the Iron Age in central Europe.

The Iron Age chronology is detailed and regional. Although the Iron Age was a pan-European phenomenon, its regional variability, together with its fragmented and tribalized cultural landscape, makes its chronology complex. In addition to typology and cross-association, the Iron Age chronology is also built upon historical events and Mediterranean imports of known date. The development of artistic styles also plays a major role in its subdivision. It is again central Europe that provided the most commonly used general chronology. The Hallstatt Period, named after an artifact-rich cemetery next to late Bronze and Iron Age salt mines in the Austrian Salzkammergut, is divided into Early (Ha A–B) and Late (Ha C–D) phases, with the former marking the end of the Urnfield culture in Europe and the latter being the first phase of the Iron Age in areas such as central and southern Europe, but the transition to the Iron Age in other regions.

The second phase of the Iron Age, when it extended throughout Europe, is named after La Tène, a site at Lake Neuchâtel in Switzerland. The exact function of this site is not known, but it contained thousands of swords, spears, shields, fibulae, and tools. These were distinctive in shape and beautifully ornamented in a style different from that of the objects from the Hallstatt period. This, the La Tène style, was found from the 5th to the 1st century BC throughout most of Europe, and its development and change over time are the basis of the chronological division into La Tène A–D. Other evidence, such as southern imports, has increasingly become incorporated into the La Tène chronology, and the time from the end of the Hallstatt Period until the spread of the Roman Empire is

Urnfield Culture

The Late Bronze Age Urnfield culture was named after its custom of placing the cremated bones of the dead in urns. The Urnfield culture first appeared in east-central Europe and northern Italy. From the 12th century onward, however, the use of urn cemeteries, or urnfields, gradually spread to Ukraine, Sicily, Scandinavia, and across France to the Iberian peninsula—a movement perhaps associated with folk migrations. In most areas the genuine Urnfield tradition of flat graves was continued, although occasionally, the urns were covered by round barrows.

Warlike behaviour among the culture's members appears to have been intense. Settlements were normally fortified, and large supplies of beaten-bronze armaments have been found. The slashing sword, with flanged grips to protect the handle, was apparently adopted at this time. The uniformity of the Urnfield culture and the persistence of certain pottery and metal forms seemingly had great influence on the later culture of the Early Iron Age.

divided into a number of short phases, each with distinct material expressions. The stylistic basis of this chronology stresses the common heritage, the Celtic art style, which developed over large areas of Europe during this time.

CHARACTERISTICS OF THE COPPER AGE

Also known as the Chalcolithic or Eneolithic Period, the Copper Age was a time of diffuse and sporadic use of copper for a limited number of small tools and personal ornaments. If the age is defined simply as the time when copper first began to be used, then localized Copper Age cultures existed in southeastern Europe from the 5th millennium BC. On the other hand, if it is defined as the time when copper was an established element in the material culture, then it must be dated from about 3200 BC in the Carpathian basin and southeastern Europe, slightly later in the Aegean, and later still in Iberia.

In these early copper-using societies, copper had no importance in subsistence production, and the tools made could hardly compete with those of flint and stone. The new material had prestige, however, and was used to adorn the deceased. It was at this early stage of metal use that one of its important roles was established: to mark and articulate social prestige and status. The Copper Age as a distinct stage developed only in a few regions, including groups in areas as far apart as Bulgaria, Bohemia, the Aegean, and southeastern Spain.

One of these remarkable centres of early copper use was in southeastern Spain. Situated in the Almerian lowland, in an area confined by the coast and the mountains, it was a densely settled region with large nucleated and often fortified hilltop settlements of surprising architectural sophistication and with a rich and inventive material culture known as the Millaran culture, after the site of Los Millares. Like contemporary sites in the region, Los Millares was located so as to overlook a river from a promontory in the foothills of higher mountains. The sides and plateau of the hill were fortified with massive stone walls, regularly placed semicircular bastions, and outlying towers. These created a well-defined and protected space of approximately 12 acres (5 hectares), with several occupation phases and of some complexity. The settlement was townlike, with rows of stone houses, alleys, and a central communal place within the walls. An artificial watercourse may have led to the settlement. There was specialization of production between households. Outside the settlement was a cemetery containing more than 100 megalithic tombs with corbeled chambers used as collective burial places.

CHARACTERISTICS OF
THE BRONZE AGE

Simultaneous with such Copper Age cultures were a number of late Neolithic cultures in other regions. The Early Bronze Age had, therefore, various roots. In some areas it developed from the Copper Age, while in others it grew out of late Neolithic cultures. In western and part of central Europe, the Bell Beaker culture continued into the Early Bronze Age. It had introduced the use of copper for prestigious personal objects, individual burial rites, and possibly also new ideological structures to the Neolithic societies over vast areas of Europe. These new elements were the basis of the transformation that took place during the Early Bronze Age and became prominent within the emerging societies.

In the rest of central and in northern Europe, the Corded Ware culture was an important component of the late Neolithic, and some local Early Bronze Age characteristics can be traced to these roots. For example, this is seen in terms of burial rituals. Burials of the Corded Ware culture were usually single graves in pits, with or without a barrow. The deceased was placed in a contracted position, men on their left side, women on their right, both facing south. This differentiation of body position according to sex was maintained in the earliest Bronze Age in many areas, but at times the orientation was reversed, such as at Branč, in Slovakia, where 81 percent of females were on their left side and 61 percent of males on their right. As the period progressed, grave forms began to diversify, and, though inhumation in pits remained the commonest form, it was elaborated in different ways. The position of the body became stretched rather than contracted, and sex and age were not expressed by body position but were reflected through elements such as grave goods or location within the cemetery.

The characteristics of, and the dates for, the Early
Bronze Age vary regionally in central Europe. Some areas,
such as the Saarland, even appear either to have had continuous Neolithic occupation until as late as 1400 BC or to
have been uninhabited during the Early Bronze Age. Most
of these areas were enclaves, however, and it was only in
Scandinavia, where the Bronze Age began about 1800 BC,
that the transition to the Bronze Age was substantially
delayed for a whole region.

Such local delay of the earliest Bronze Age cannot
simply be seen in terms of retarded cultural development.
Rather, it reflects that different cultural trajectories were
followed by various societies. Scandinavia illustrates this
well, since the period preceding the Bronze Age was a
time not of devolution but of new flint technologies and
new material forms, with a wealth of beautifully manufactured flint daggers and a conspicuous display of local
craft. This constituted a distinct local Late Neolithic
phase, interspersed between the Corded Ware culture
and the Bronze Age proper. The flint daggers show clear
influences from bronze daggers, and examples of flint
swords reflect the emulation of new ideas. This indicates the degree of contact with bronze-using societies.
When bronze was introduced and incorporated into the
local culture, its role in terms of the cultural manners of
manufacture and behaviour was rapidly established, and
it quickly reflected a distinct local tradition: the Nordic
Bronze Age. At this point, the absence of local raw material did not prevent the society from integrating bronze
as a basic material in its culture nor did the dependency
on trade partners for bronze mean that the local material
culture developed without its own distinct character. The
Nordic Bronze Age illustrates the ability of local cultures
to maintain their independent character in spite of dependency on other, larger systems. This characteristic can be

observed in different forms throughout the Metal Ages, and, in an essential manner, this qualifies the impression of an overall common cultural heritage developing during these millennia.

Although the dates and the cultural roots of the Early Bronze Age vary, it is similarly defined by the use of copper alloys for tools throughout Europe. During the Bronze Age, the techniques of metalworking increased in sophistication. A range of new working methods, such as valve molds, cire perdue, and sheet-metal working, were developed. The development of molds made it possible both to mass-produce objects and to produce more elaborate items, including hollow objects. One of the most spectacular objects produced in this fashion was the lur, a musical instrument of great precision and beauty. The later Bronze Age and Iron Age method of sheet working facilitated the production of large objects, such as caldrons and shields, and a similar working method was used for the boss motif of bands of raised circles, which became a favoured element on many Urnfield Period objects such as horse harnesses and situlae (bucket-shaped vessels).

The manner of decorating the objects expressed regional as well as chronological styles. Among these, the most noticeable stylistic developments were the widespread use of the combined sun-bird-ship motif of the Urnfield culture and the later break in stylistic tradition indicated by La Tène, or so-called Celtic, art. Most important, however, may be the invention of new types of objects. While objects made of ceramics, gold, stone, and organic materials during this period differed from those of previous periods, they did not represent drastic changes in the employment of a particular medium, but this was not true of bronze. Bronze is an artificial material made by alloying copper with different metals, in particular tin, through which a new material with its own

Prehistoric Italian votive plate showing an Iron Age warrior in full battle regalia, including a spear and a large defensive shield. A. Dagli Orti/De Agostini Picture Library/Getty Images

distinct properties is produced. The production of bronze was an invention in its true sense, and the potentials of this material were increasingly revealed and exploited during the Bronze Age. The effect of this was a range of new objects, of which some were new shapes for old concepts but others introduced new functions and concepts into the societies.

Among the latter, one of the most important new elements was the invention of the sword. With the sword there was for the first time in European history an object entirely dedicated to fighting and not doubling as a tool. Fighting is evident from earlier periods as well, but during the Bronze Age it was formalized. Toward the Late Bronze Age the warrior emerged, sheathed in an assemblage of defensive items: the armour. To have been a warrior during the Iron Age must have been an established role, and the importance of warfare led to monumental defensive structures and further evolution of swords and shields. The latter development shows changes in the fighting technique, and in the Early Iron Age the stabbing sword of the Bronze Age was replaced by a heavy slashing sword, indicating fighting from horseback. The actual importance of warfare is difficult to establish, and a distinction between the symbolic representation of aggression and real aggression must be kept in mind. The presence of swords and armour does, however, represent a concrete expression of aggression and of the concept of warfare.

The increased importance of fortified settlements and villages further shows that aggression was a major component of life. Professional soldiers, as they were known at the time of the Roman Empire and the Middle Ages, are unlikely to have existed at this time, but group warfare existed from the Iron Age onward, and other related professions developed. For example, the location of fortified sites in strategic places, such as near mountain passes and

Bell Beaker Culture

The Late Neolithic–Early Bronze Age people known as the Bell Beaker, or Beaker, culture lived about 4,500 years ago in the temperate zones of Europe. They received their name from their distinctive bell-shaped beakers, decorated in horizontal zones by finely toothed stamps. The graves of the Beaker folk were usually modest single units, though in much of western Europe they often took the form of megalithic tombs. A warlike stock, they were primarily bowmen but were also armed with a flat, tanged dagger or spearhead of copper, and a curved, rectangular wrist guard. Their extensive search for copper (and gold), in fact, greatly accelerated the spread of bronze metallurgy in Europe. Probably originally from Spain, the Beaker folk soon spread into central and western Europe in their search for metals. In central Europe they came into contact with the Battle-Ax (or Single-Grave) culture, which was also characterized by beaker-shaped pottery (though different in detail) and by the use of horses and a shaft-hole battle-ax. The two cultures gradually intermixed and later spread from central Europe to eastern England.

Beaker found at Denton, Lincolnshire, Eng. Courtesy of the trustees of the British Museum

river crossings, suggests that these sites were not primarily defensive but were based on the ability to control certain resources, including access and passage. This is illustrated by the rich Early Bronze Age fortified site at Spišský Štvrtok, Slovakia, strategically located to control the trade routes running through a mountain pass across the Carpathians along the Hornád River, and by the Late Bronze Age the Lusatian hilltop site in the Moravian Pforte passes. The development of aggression and its formalization played a role in providing middlemen and entrepreneurs with opportunities and helped to establish them in the position of power they gained in the Iron Age.

CHARACTERISTICS OF THE IRON AGE

During most of the Middle and Late Bronze Age, iron was present, albeit scarce. It was used for personal ornaments and small knives, for repairs on bronzes, and for bimetallic items. The Iron Age thus did not start with the first appearance of iron but rather at the stage when its distinct functional properties were being exploited and it began to supplant bronze in the production of tools and weapons. This occurred at different times in various parts of Europe, and the transition to the Iron Age is embedded in local cultural developments. The reasons why iron was adopted differed among regions, but generally a similar pattern was followed. After an introductory period, iron quickly supplanted bronze for the making of tools and weapons. It was at this stage that metal, in spite of the earlier presence of bronze tools, replaced stone, flint, and wood in agricultural production. New and more effective tools were developed during the last centuries BC, and subsistence production must have increased drastically. Along with these domestic changes, there were changes in the traditional routes of contact and trade. These routes had been established during the Bronze Age, and through them copper, tin, and other commodities had traveled throughout Europe. With the appearance of the rich Late Hallstatt communities of south-central Europe, the orientation of contact changed. The northern links were increasingly ignored, and trade became concentrated on, and dependent upon, commodities from the south. South and west-central Europe were now included in the periphery of the expanding Mediterranean civilization, and the previous network of contact was broken. In the rest of Europe, regional diversity increased, a tribalized landscape emerged, and new types of social organization developed. During the Iron Age, the roots of historic Europe were planted. Proto-urban settlements, hierarchical social orders, new ideological structures, and writing were parts of this picture. It was also a time during which the difference between the Mediterranean world and temperate Europe became even more pronounced and new degrees and forms of dependency developed in the sociopolitical systems.

SOCIAL AND ECONOMIC DEVELOPMENTS

The transitions between the three phases of the Metal Ages are primarily defined by a change in the metal used, but they also reflect economic changes and transformations of social organization. It is within these larger concerns that the character of this part of European prehistory can be found.

CONTROL OVER RESOURCES

The Metal Ages were periods of discovery, invention, and exploitation of various metals and metallurgical procedures. New elements were introduced into the societies, which played a role in their further development. In the later 5th and earlier 4th millennia BC, copper from easily worked surface deposits was used for relatively simple items in southeastern Europe and the Carpathian basin.

The Transylvanian copper ores were particularly important. For example, copper was extracted from the quarry at Varna, Bulg., about 4400 BC in an area near a rich Copper Age cemetery. After this initial exploitation, metal objects again became rare until they reappeared in the late 4th millennium BC. The reasons for this change are unknown but may in part relate to the depletion of surface ore deposits. At this early state, the technique of copper manufacture consisted of smelting in an open one-faced mold and hammering.

Later, when copper of different compositions from deeper deposits was used, the properties of copper in combination with other metals were explored. The copper sulfide ores from these deep mines were more difficult to procure, since they relied on more sophisticated mining techniques and needed initial roasting before smelting. At the same time, they were more widely available than surface deposits, and there were sources in both central and western Europe—ores in Germany, Austria, and the Czech and Slovak Republics were exploited from the early 3rd millennium BC. This long initial phase of sporadic use of copper was finally replaced by a period of copper alloys, which began about 2500 BC in southeastern Europe, slightly later in the Aegean, and later still in Iberia.

Bronze industries were widespread in Europe by 2300 BC, but copper-tin alloys were first used toward the end of the 3rd millennium, with renewal of the centres of metallurgical production in Austria, Germany, and neighbouring areas. The raw material needed was available only in a few regions, and tin, particularly restricted in its distribution, was found only in eastern Portugal, Sardinia, Tuscany, Cornwall, the Isles of Scilly, and the Bohemian Ore Mountains. The latter site, on the border between the Czech Republic and eastern Germany, was one of the rare instances of close proximity between copper and tin. This region, together with the copper areas of the Harz Mountains, the Alps, and central Slovakia, became one of the most important regions of the Early Bronze Age. With the progression of the Bronze Age, local metallurgical traditions developed throughout Europe, including areas lacking both tin and copper sources, but the chief metalworking centres continued to influence the material culture of larger areas. This was an important factor behind the trade and exchange network that came into existence.

The discovery of iron was most likely a by-product of bronze working, and much of the earliest iron use is not culturally distinct from the use of bronze. At its early stage, iron may have been monopolized and produced by those individuals or groups who controlled bronze. Iron, however, is different from bronze in many respects. It is found widely in Europe either as iron ore or as bog iron. To be usable, iron does not need alloying with other metals, and the demands are mainly the fuel and labour needed to smelt or roast the ore. This process involves high temperatures and skilled control of pyrotechnology. To produce a usable iron, the bloom must be hammered while red-hot to reduce the impurities and to change its internal structures. Only then can the shaping of the final object begin. Thus, the production of an iron object consists of several distinct stages, each different from those involved in bronze production.

Iron appeared in Romania about 1700 BC and in Greece shortly after. During the Middle and Late Bronze Age, it occurred infrequently except in Iberia, Britain, and some other parts of western Europe. The earliest iron was used for small knives, pins, and other personal objects and for repairs on bronze items. Only in Romania was iron used for heavy tools during the Bronze Age; toward the end of the Bronze Age, tools and some weapons made of iron appeared generally in Europe. With Ha C, iron swords were being made, and, in the following La Tène Period, iron had clearly become a material important in its own right, being used for a range of new functional items, including plowshares, carpentry tools, and nails. At this point it is likely that the previous monopolies on metal production and trade were severely challenged, and iron became a common material, produced and procured anywhere in Europe.

The intensity of metal use varied regionally, and the centres of innovation and wealth moved over time. During the Metal Ages the communities of Europe can be studied through their reaction to, and adoption of, their inventions. It is a phase in prehistory that raises cultural questions about the nature of innovation and of its consequences for society. Metal brought several important new items to the communities, but, more importantly, it changed the nature of society itself. The production of bronze was an important step in human history, indicating a point at which the limits imposed by natural materials were broken by human invention. The behavioral impact of this cannot be measured, but it was likely substantial. It may have altered attitudes to nature, creating the activities that resulted in deep mining of metals and salt, and caused experimentation with new materials, such as glass.

Metal also had social impact, and one of its important roles came from its involvement in the articulation of prestige and status and thus its ability to assign power. Scarcity usually implies preciousness, and control over scarce or precious resources often leads to power. The production of both bronze and iron objects involved scarcity of either resources or knowledge or both. Control of metal production was a relevant factor in prehistory, as shown by the location of important Copper Age and Early Bronze Age communities in close proximity to copper or tin ores or by the breakdown of trade alliances that occurred in the Early Iron Age. The wealth and outstanding material culture of the Copper and Early Bronze Age communities were probably related to the trade in, and prestigious value of, copper and bronze. It is also a characteristic of these communities that this wealth was not consolidated by other activities, and some of the centres were short-lived and declined quickly. The lack of ability to invest and rechannel wealth in absolute terms is one of the most basic differences between these communities and those of both the Mediterranean civilizations and the Iron Age. Only some of the Copper Age centres developed into flourishing communities in the earliest Bronze Age. Those that did remain became the Early Bronze Age centres of wealth, contact, and trade, with dense populations. These centres were widely spaced and were internally extremely different, ranging from places such as El Argar in Iberia to Wessex in southern England. Of these, the Argaric culture in southeastern Iberia comprised nucleated village settlements similar to those from Los Millares but with even greater sophistication and with a changed funerary rite. The deceased, richly adorned with diadems, arm rings, and pins and accompanied by metal tools, were individually entombed in large funerary urns placed under the house floors. At the other extreme was the group of rich Early Bronze Age graves in Wessex. The objects found in them are comparable in wealth to the Argaric ones, and, although the exotic items were unique to each area, they shared a range of tools and some ornaments. There was essential divergence in other respects, however, and at Wessex there was no association with elaborate domestic structures. The rich graves served as the ritual centre for a dispersed community living in relatively simple constructions of wattle and daub and without demarcations of the limits of their settlements. These Early Bronze Age centres developed in different environmental zones, ranging from semiarid to lush temperate, and they are at different distances from copper ore. They all have possible links with areas containing tin ores, however, and they developed in regions that were local centres in the previous period. These two criteria may have been necessary conditions for this development, but such conditions in themselves did not result in rich centres in the Early Bronze Age, nor could they guarantee continuous survival of the centres. As in the case of the earlier Copper Age centres, these were without an additional stable foundation, and they disappeared at different rates and under varying local circumstances. Such situations were plentiful during the Metal Ages. They show not only that the scarce and prestigious resources could be controlled and could give access to power and wealth but also that a multitude of factors influenced whether that power was secured and how it was maintained.

CHANGING CENTRES OF WEALTH

Societies are dynamic structures that interact with each other. In this interaction, asymmetrical relationships frequently develop between areas or groups, with one partner assuming a central, and the other a peripheral, role. Such relations are not stable, however, and over time their internal asymmetry will change. These changes can be illustrated by two examples from the Metal Ages in western central Europe.

The first is from the Early Bronze Age, where a remarkable shift in cultural initiative took place. The earliest Bronze Age centre, Unetician A, consisted of a complex of flat inhumation graves with modest grave goods in copper and bronze that was found in Slovakia. During Unetician B this complex continued, spreading into Bohemia and much of Germany and Poland. In this process, the original centre was complemented by a number of extremely rich graves on its periphery, such as at Leubingen, Helmsdorf, and Straubing in central Germany and Łęki Małe in southern Poland. These graves were inhumations under large barrows, with elaborate chambers and rich grave goods. Leubingen, for example, was a 28-foot- (8.5-metre-) high barrow with an elaborately constructed 66-foot-wide (20.1-metre-wide) central stone cairn delineated by a ring ditch. The cairn covered and protected a thatched tentlike wooden structure made of large oak planks with gypsum mortar in the cracks. The skeleton of an old man lay extended on the oak floor, and at a right angle across his hips lay another body, which appeared to be that of an adolescent or child. In the space around the deceased were a number of objects, including, a pot in a setting of stones, bronze halberds and tools, and a group of gold ornaments. These graves show that a new and radically different funerary ceremony had taken place in this area, although the material culture still remained related to that of the previous centre. Thus, this group of barrows constituted a complementary Unetician area on the periphery of the original complex, and it was from this area that much of the impetus for the development of the Tumulus Period came.

The second illustration of change in the relationship between areas is from the earliest Iron Age in southern Germany, as exemplified by the hill fort at Heuneburg and its satellite barrows and secondary sites. These sites show how the central position of southern Germany and Switzerland during the Urnfield Period was transformed in the course of the Late Hallstatt Period into a peripheral role on the edge of the Mediterranean world. Heuneburg had several occupation phases, ranging from the middle of the 2nd millennium BC to the late 1st millennium AD, but the climax of its occupation was in the 6th and early 5th centuries BC, the so-called IV phase. The site, on a promontory overlooking the valley of the upper Danube, consisted of 7 acres (2.83 hectares) enclosed within a defensive earthwork. During its IV phase, this defense included bastions and mud-brick walls, both of which were Mediterranean inventions. The site was densely populated, and it shows a range of activities taking place at the interior in workshops for bronze, iron, antler, and coral. Among the imports were Black-Figure shards from Greece, an Etruscan clay mold, and wine amphorae from a Greek colony in southern France. Some of the local pottery, which was among the earliest wheel-thrown pottery in central Europe, shows imitation of Greek ornamentation from southern France, while other examples copy Etruscan bronze vessels.

On the plateau behind Heuneburg are several large barrows with multiple burials, which are among the largest and richest in Europe. There were a number of farmsteads between these and the hill fort itself. This association between an important hill fort and rich graves for male and female leaders was present at other places during the 6th and early 5th centuries BC, particularly in eastern France, Switzerland, and southwestern Germany. Examples include the Hohenasperg oppidum and the rich burials at Kleinaspergle, in southern Germany, and the Mont Lassois oppidum in eastern France and the Vix grave. The latter contained a five-foot-high (1.52 metre-high) bronze wine krater of Greco-Etruscan workmanship, a gold diadem, and an exquisite bronze statuette, together with wine-drinking equipment, Greek pottery, a vehicle, and other ornaments. The complexity of the structural buildup in the landscape surrounding these hill forts is amazing. Many of the sites had several phases of occupation but, as with Heuneburg, the Late Hallstatt Period is a distinct phase, and the brief time it took for these centres to come into existence demonstrates the potential for power available at the time.

Heuneburg was one of the wealthiest of all these sites, and it is important for many reasons. It provides evidence of emulation of another culture, and it clearly demonstrates the changes in its position vis-à-vis a number of cultural systems. This is shown most clearly in the construction techniques used in phase IV, which copied both plans and building techniques from Greece. The mud bricks were totally unsuited to this part of Europe, but they show the importance of the Mediterranean culture during this period, as does the adoption of wine-drinking ceremonies. Through these evidences of emulation, Heuneburg stands as a key site for appreciating the changes in the Early Iron Age in the relationship between the Classical world and the rest of Europe.

The exceptional concentration of Late Hallstatt chieftain burials on the upper Danube and upper Rhine lasted only to the beginning of the 5th century BC, when decentralization set in, but it had played a role in a period when relations within Europe were transformed. During the Bronze Age, Europe was roughly divided into two worlds: the eastern Mediterranean and temperate Europe, each with a common cultural heritage. With the Iron Age, the fragmentation and diversification of temperate Europe began, while the eastern Mediterranean expanded through a burst of colonial activities that resulted in cultural dominance over an extended but internally diverse area.

PRESTIGE AND STATUS

The Neolithic was a period of remarkable communal enterprises. Against this background, the emphasis that the Bell Beaker and Corded Ware cultures placed on the individual constituted a radical change. The British archaeologist Colin Renfrew characterized the change as one from "group orientation" to "individualized chiefdom," and this change was essential for the emerging Early Bronze Age communities. In the Late Neolithic, collective burials disappear from European prehistory in favour of individual graves. The form of the grave and the character of the funerary ceremonies changed substantially during the Bronze and Iron ages. The common and widespread use of cremation introduced by the Urnfield culture is an important indication of the potential for radical changes within this realm. Throughout the period, the individual remained the focus of the funerary ceremony, and the evidence suggests that prestige and status often were communicated through the wealth and types of objects found in graves. It is debated whether the differences between individuals that this suggests were classlike and absolute, were expressions of sex, age, and lineage differentiation, or were assigned through deeds rather than ascribed at birth. The changes through time suggest increased social differentiation, but there also are periods, such as the Urnfield culture, in which social differentiations are less obviously expressed in graves. The grave can, therefore, be used mainly to establish relative differentiation within one community rather than pronouncing absolute historical trends. One such study comes from the cemetery at Brenč, where 308 inhumation graves spanning 200 to 400 years of the early Unetician culture were analyzed. Within the graves there was clear evidence of internal differentiation, with some individuals having more elaborate grave goods than others. This suggests that in this type of community there would be leading families, marked by their grave goods, and that wealth and status would tend to be inherited through the male line (since male children had richer grave goods than female children). Females obtained rich costumes during adolescence and young adulthood, possibly at the time of their marriage. The status expressed at this period was to a large extent relational, placing each member of the community according to lineage, sex, and age. This differentiation was not directly based on access to power, possessions, or absolute wealth, and, in most areas of temperate Europe, social differentiation until the 1st millennium BC was likely moderate. The exception to this was short-lived local expressions of individual wealth or, more likely, prestige, such as the Wessex graves and the Leubingen-Helmsdorf group, which suggest single leaders occupying sociopolitical roles that were symbolized through emblems of power.

Throughout the Bronze Age, sex and age were the main components organizing the structures of daily life. Outside the Mediterranean area, there were few differences between the size and plan of most of the structures within individual sites, although the sites within a region often were internally ranked in terms of size and complexity, which suggests that they had different functions. Such "tiered" settlement systems came into being in the Early Bronze Age in areas such as southeastern Europe, and they were quite prominent during the Late Bronze Age in the Lusatian culture of Poland and northeastern Germany as well as in the Urnfield culture of central Europe. This settlement organization probably continued into the Early Iron Age in some regions, such as England, where the hill forts became central places for an agricultural, and possibly also political, upland.

A clear social and political hierarchy was, however, lacking from the Bronze Age settlement pattern. This was particularly true of northern, western, and central Europe, which saw a variety of settlement organizations during the period. There were extended farmsteads in northern and western Europe with a development of enclosed compounds and elaborate field systems in Britain. In central Europe the extended farmsteads were in time supplemented by both unenclosed villages and defended hilltop sites, as was also the case in the area of the Late Bronze Age Lusatian complex in Poland and neighbouring areas. The fortified settlements were usually large planned enterprises, rather than organic village sprawl, and they were often erected over a few years; an example is the Lusatian defended settlement at Biskupin, Pol., where a settlement of 102–106 houses estimated to shelter some 1,000 to 1,200 people was built in just one year. The fortified sites and enclosed villages of the European Bronze Age show centralized decision-making and capacities for planning and constructing grand enterprises. Their concern was the whole community rather than the individual household, and communal features such as paths, gates, and wells were well maintained and planned. The superbly preserved Late Bronze Age sites from the Swiss lakes show these communities vividly. The settlement at Cortallois-Est, on Lake Neuchâtel in Switzerland, illustrates the main features of such sites: straight rows of equal-sized houses aligning paths and alleyways, with the whole complex contained within a perimeter fence. Each house had a fireplace with a decorated house-alter, or firedog. The rubbish accumulated in front of the entrance, and various activities took place within the house. The sites were densely inhabited, and minor internal differences of objects and structure existed between the houses, but they were not divided into different classes in terms of their wealth, size, or accessibility, although different crafts and trades may have made up quarters within the village. These Late Bronze Age villages did not contain any structures that could be interpreted as administrative centres or religious offices.

A different form of organization is found throughout the Early Bronze Age in southeastern Europe and in southeastern Spain. Both areas had nucleated defended settlements during this period, and there appears to have been some differentiation of the houses in terms of function and size. A tendency toward centralization is demonstrated by the Early Bronze Age site at Spišsky Štvrtok. This was a fortified site of economic, administrative, and strategic importance. An oval area,

An etching of a fortified village in Biskupin, Pol. The large fence surrounding the village provided protection from marauding invaders. Johannes Simon/ Getty Images

enclosed by a ditch and rampart, was differentiated into an acropolis and a settlement area, with the houses of the acropolis built using a different technique. The amount of gold and bronze objects hidden in chests under the floors of the houses in the settlement area further suggests that there were economic and social distinctions among the inhabitants.

The important exception to this picture is the eastern Mediterranean, which underwent a rapid and dramatic social development during this period, permanently severing its cultural affinity with temperate Europe. At a time of modest stratification in the rest of Europe, the first European civilization—as defined by administration, bookkeeping, writing, urbanism, and the separation of different kinds of power—arose in the Aegean. Its background was the Neolithic cultures of the 3rd millennium BC, which were closely aligned with those of temperate and southeastern Europe. The Neolithic roots alone cannot explain the development in the Aegean, and there is no convincing evidence for external influences behind these changes in Greece, nor is there basis for arguing for a migration. Local factors must have caused development to follow a different route in this area.

One of many possible factors was the marked population increase in the south Aegean during the Early Bronze Age. This led to the development of some extensive settlements, although the overall settlement pattern continued to be dispersed, with a majority of small hamlets and farmsteads. This could have caused a degree of settlement hierarchy at this stage, with some sites acting as regional centres. Central places provide opportunity for craft specialization and redistribution of commodities and thus lead to social hierarchy and a type of society known as the complex chiefdom. Another important factor was the change in agricultural production that followed the adoption of vine and olive cultivation during the 3rd millennium BC and the possible increase in the exploitation of sheep. These were commodity-oriented activities, which furthered exchange and redistribution. These products were more suitable for a redistributive economy than for a household economy. Olives, in particular, demand capital investment, since it takes several years before the crop produces. Within this setting, the palace economy, a complex bureaucratic organization based on a redistributive economy, developed. The first state had thus appeared in Europe.

This process can be followed from 1800 BC onward in Mycenae, in mainland Greece, and on Crete. The character of the society was distinct at each of these centres, but the palace economy distinguished them from the villages and farmsteads of temperate Europe. For reasons not clearly known but possibly related to subsistence crises and over-exploitation of dwindling metal supplies, these centres collapsed suddenly about 1200 BC, and thereafter Greece entered its Dark Ages. After a few centuries of restructuring, about 800 BC this was followed by a remarkable Greek expansion into the western Mediterranean, during which colonies were founded in southern Italy, Mediterranean France (Massalia), and along the southeastern coast of Spain. The Etruscan state, which developed in Italy from about 700 BC, competed for domination of the western Mediterranean, and during the Early Iron Age Etruscan as well as Greek influences reached beyond their Mediterranean neighbours.

During the Iron Age, stratification became common and marked throughout Europe. Differences in wealth and status in terms of both individuals and households were reflected in graves as well as settlements. Settlements reveal internal division of houses according to size and function, and the population of any village was divided by wealth in addition to sex, age, kinship, and personal characteristics. Socially differentiated settlements existed from Scandinavia to Italy and from Ireland to the Russian borders, although they were differently laid out and organized. This period saw the building of permanent fences and enclosures around fields and farms; the development of villages and, within these, increasing differentiation of the sizes of individual buildings; and increased stratification between settlements, with proto-urban centres coming into being. The rate of change varied in different parts of Europe, but toward the end of the 1st millennium BC all areas had undergone these changes. The end of this trend in northern Europe is vividly illustrated by the Hodde village in Denmark, where the community can be followed during the centuries near the end of the 1st millennium, revealing how a few farms within the enclosed village gradually grew bigger at the cost of the others. An unstratified village was replaced by a society divided into rich and poor in only a few centuries. In other parts of temperate Europe, social division was equally clearly present, and proto-urban characteristics such as commerce, administrative centres, and religious offices came into existence on some of these sites. In this process, the defended hilltop settlement of the Early Iron Age was increasingly replaced by more complex sites.

The proto-urban tendencies are particularly strongly suggested by the oppida of western, central, and eastern Europe. These were often densely populated enclosed sites, which housed full-time specialists, such as glassmakers, leather workers, and smiths. Manching, one of the largest oppida in Europe, contained many of these characteristics. The site, located at the junction of the Danube and the Paar rivers, was occupied from about 200 BC and developed rapidly from a small undefended village to a large walled settlement. The defense was an elaborate construction consisting of four-mile-long (6.43 kilometres) walls built of timber and stones and including four gateways. Some areas within the defense were never occupied, but others (a total of about 500 acres, or 202.3 hectares) were densely settled. The organization of the settlement was preplanned, with streets up to 30 feet wide (9.14 metres) and regular rows of rectangular buildings in front of zones containing pits and working areas; other areas were enclosed for granaries or the stalling of horses. The site was divided into work areas for particular crafts, such as wood, leather, and iron working. Coins were minted and used on the site, and there is evidence of much trade.

A market economy, rather than a redistributive economy, is the hallmark of these sites, and they were important supplements to the regionally dispersed smaller villages and farmsteads. Commodities became direct wealth, and the exchange of different values was monitored through coins. A drastically altered society was the result, but the Roman expansion at the end of the 2nd century BC caused major changes and brought local development to an end. The Romans established their own towns and a new system of government, and the oppida were not given the opportunity of developing on their own into towns, for which they had laid the ground.

The beginning of the Iron Age was in many areas marked by change in burial rites. The extensive use of cremation during the Urnfield Period was replaced by inhumation graves with magnificent displays of wealth. During the Late Hallstatt Period these changes were most dramatically reflected by the group of so-called princely graves in west-central Europe. These were immensely rich burials in large barrows, in which the construction of grave chamber and barrow became monumental enterprises, reminiscent of the late Unetician barrows at Leubingen and Straubing. In each case the grave was a display of power and status, giving emphasis and prestige to an individual or a lineage at a time of overt disruption of the social order. One of these rich Hallstatt graves was Hohmichele, located within the complex around Heuneburg on the Danube. This barrow was one of the satellite graves surrounding the large hill fort. It covered a central grave and 12 secondary burials. The barrow was constructed in several stages, resulting in a large imposing monument on the level land behind the hill fort. The central grave was robbed in antiquity, but it had been an inhumation grave within a wood-lined chamber, which acted as the display area for the wealth of the deceased. The walls seem to have been draped in textiles with thin gold bands, and the deceased, dressed in finery including silk, was placed on a bed next to a four-wheeled wagon. These graves, while commemorating members of the society in a traditional way, also show new elements that had become part of the life of the nobility north of the Alps. The drinking set suggests the adoption and importance of the Greek drinking ceremonies, using the Greek jugs and *Schnabelkannen* ("beaked pots") for pouring and serving wine, the kraters for mixing, and the amphorae for storage and transport. The implied wine-drinking ceremony, which was likely restricted to certain sectors of the society, and furniture directly imported from the south show the emulation of southern city life by the central European chiefs.

The rich princely graves were constructed in southwestern Germany during Ha C–D. Thereafter inhumation graves became more widespread in central Europe and neighbouring areas, and they were the main burial form until the 2nd century BC, when formal burial rites disappeared in many regions and cremation was reintroduced in others. The graves of the early La Tène Period remained very rich, but barrows and elaborate grave chambers ceased after their resurrection by the Hallstatt princes and princesses. Regional variations in rites and assemblages became prolific. In France, La Tène cemeteries contained rich flat graves that had two-wheeled wagons rather than the earlier four-wheeled ones. These graves held large amounts of beautifully manufactured Celtic objects such as swords and torques, as well as Roman and Greek imports, and there were clear distinctions drawn between the sexes. In central and eastern Europe a new regional complex had developed northwest of the Black Sea, in which there were both inhumation and cremation graves clustered in large cemeteries. This complex is often attributed to Scythian invaders, and the rich assemblages and warrior graves show their influence. In the area of the lower reaches of the Dnieper, Dniester, and Don rivers, rich Scythian graves have been excavated in the form of shaft and pit graves; in these, the deceased was accompanied by a number of other humans and by horse burials. In northern Europe and Scandinavia, cremation in large urnfields continued during most of the Iron Age. In this area the social differentiation present in the settlements and the wealth displayed by a few large hoards were not expressed in the graves, and, while large numbers of the population were given formal burials, their social statuses were not explicitly expressed in this ritual. Roman and Greek imports and wine-drinking ceremonies also reached northern Europe, but it was not until the end of the Iron Age, when formal inhumation burials reappeared, that they were being used in ways similar to those in more southerly regions.

In Britain the sequence is even more complicated and shows both a strong indigenous tradition and clear local influences from western Europe. The greatest complication is the disappearance of formal burials in this area in the Late Bronze Age; they did not reappear before the last century BC and then only in a few regions, such as Yorkshire. The Late Iron Age inhumation graves in Yorkshire are almost identical to wagon graves in northern France, and there must have been very specific and personal contacts between the two areas to account for this.

Social differentiation existed throughout the Metal Ages but changed with time and in degree. This was not, however, a smooth process that can easily be followed through the centuries. There were odd kinks in the progression from the minimal ranking of the earliest Bronze Age to the proto-urban state of the Late Iron Age. There were also spatial variabilities and a number of different factors involved in the progression toward greater social complexity. Throughout the Metal Ages in Europe, new social institutions came into being and the relationships between people changed.

THE RELATIONSHIP BETWEEN NATURE AND CULTURE

During the Middle Bronze Age, the landscapes of most parts of Europe were filled in. Nature became cultivated, and this had costs. It seriously affected social organization as the population spread over larger areas and adapted to local conditions. It also affected the environment, which during the later part of the Bronze Age began to change. This was in part due to climatic changes, but it was furthered by human activity. There was overexploitation of marginal lands, and people had moved onto the dunes in areas such as Poland and The Netherlands and into the uplands of Britain, France, and Scandinavia. But, even on less marginal land, centuries of agricultural exploitation began to exact a price. Many areas in southeastern Europe were extensively overpopulated in comparison with their agricultural capacities in the Copper and Early Bronze ages. In Hungary, for example, the area around the large Early Bronze Age tell at Tószeg was so densely occupied that the villages were within sight of each other. Overpopulation and overexploitation caused peat formation to begin, heathland to expand, blanket bog to grow over established fields and grazing grounds, and fields to turn into meadows. How the people reacted to this is not known in detail, nor is it easy to establish the rate of change, but it is possible to detect a number of changes during the end of the Bronze Age and the Early Iron Age that were associated with the strained economic and ecological conditions. These changes in the environment were not, as previously believed, an environmental catastrophe, but humans had influenced their surroundings to such an extent that they had to change their way of life in order to live with the consequences.

RITUALS, RELIGION, AND ART

Throughout this period there were vivid and striking manifestations of religious beliefs, ritual behaviour, and artistic activities. One of the most remarkable phenomena was hoarding. Objects, usually in large numbers, were deliberately hidden in the ground or deposited in water in the form of a hoard. Hoards were known in a modest form during the Neolithic Period, and in some areas, such as Scandinavia and France, there continued to be a few large hoards in the Iron Age; but it was in the Bronze Age that hoarding became a common phenomenon of great social and economic importance. The contents of the hoards varied; they ranged from two to several hundred items or consisted of only one deliberately deposited object, such as the single swords found in the River Thames. They might contain several objects of the same type or of many different types. They were commonly placed in association with wet areas—such as rivers, bogs, and meadows—or located under or near large stones, including in old megalithic tombs. They were seldom parts of settlements, but they have been found in wells, such as at Berlin-Lichterfelde, in Germany. They also may have come to function as a foundation deposit for a later settlement, as was the case at Danebury, in southern England, where an Iron Age hill fort was placed at the location of a Late Bronze Age hoard. Hoards were relatively infrequent during the earliest part of the Bronze Age, when they were found mainly in southeastern Europe, Bavaria, and Austria and contained flat axes and neck rings. Hoarding reached its peak during the later part of the Early Bronze Age and the Middle Bronze Age, when the activity spread throughout Europe and became an established phenomenon in most of its communities. In the Middle and Late Bronze Age, large numbers of hoards were deposited, and a substantial number of bronze objects were in this way consumed and withdrawn from circulation. Late Bronze Age hoards from Romania, among the largest ever, contained up to four tons of bronze objects. At the same time, large collections of unused tools, newly taken from their molds, were deposited together in France.

Hoarding is one of the more unusual elements of Bronze Age Europe, and it is difficult to explain. The activity consumed large parts of the wealth of these societies without apparent benefits. Traditional explanations have divided them into different types with varying function. The lack of settlement association means that they were not originally foundation deposits, such as are known from the Roman period. They must, therefore, be explained either in terms of metalworking procedures or as having a ritual or religious meaning. Hoards that could have been retrieved from their hiding place have been interpreted, depending on their contents, as hidden treasure, merchants' stock, or items intended for recycling by the smiths. Hoards that could not possibly have been retrieved must have had ritual or religious significance, or, alternatively, they were acts of conspicuous consumption of wealth in a potlatch ceremony. This would enhance the position of the owner and, incidentally, would also ensure the flow of imports and the value of bronze. But a functional interpretation of hoards as a kind of stock cannot account for why these hoards were so often not retrieved. Thousands of hoards were made during the Bronze Age, and enormous riches were disposed of through these activities. In spite of their internal differences and variations in terms of location, composition, and amounts, it is likely that ritual behaviour and cultural meaning were always major components of this practice. There is, however, only little indication of what that meaning was. The association with water, which became more pronounced through time, could suggest water-related rituals and has been interpreted as relating to fertility rites and agricultural production. Because the location and composition of hoards vary locally as well as through time, however, they may embody more than one meaning.

Only a few areas saw instances of hoarding in the Iron Age, and their forms were distinctly different from those of the Bronze Age. The most obvious example is the votive deposit at Hjortspring, Den., where a large wooden boat equipped for war with wooden shields, spears, and swords was destroyed and deposited in a small bog. The events behind these hoards were known to Classical writers such as Tacitus and Orosius, who gave accounts of war offerings by Germanic and Cimbrian tribes, respectively. They describe how the weaponry confiscated in war was destroyed and deposited in victory ceremonies. The Iron Age hoards of northern Europe had clear associations with war, the types and numbers of objects deposited together are incomparable with the Bronze Age hoards, and the ritual destruction of the entire assemblage was a new element.

The new hoarding ritual contained elements of conspicuous consumption, but its form and focus were different from previous activities. It developed shortly before the end of the 1st millennium, and it continued as a tradition among the Germanic tribes in northern Europe for several centuries. Another area with complex ritual ceremonies during the Iron Age is France. There are not many of these ritual places, but those that existed were large complex sanctuaries with continuous use over several centuries. One of these sites is Gournay-sur-Aronde, in northern France, a sanctuary used from 300 to 50 BC. The site consisted of a square enclosed by a ditch and palisade with a number of large pits for exposing and displaying offerings at its centre and a number of wood-lined ditches along the edges. In the ditches were found the remains of hundreds of iron weapons, all deliberately and systematically destroyed, as well as fibulae and tools. There were also the remains of 208 animals and 12 humans. These remains indicate some of the ceremonial behaviour that had taken place on the site. All cattle had the muzzle cut off during offering, and their skulls were displayed on top of pits and ditches. The humans had been beheaded, and the bones were at some points moved from the central pits to the ditches and rearranged there according to different prescriptions. The archaeology shows that both the Bronze and Iron ages were periods of specific and unique ritual behaviour but also that their beliefs and norms were not uniform throughout each period. As the socioeconomic structures of these societies changed, their ideological structures underwent transformation.

Societies reveal themselves through their art. These expressions are, however, difficult to interpret, and much of this evidence from the past has disappeared. It is at the same time an essential source, giving insight into the artistry and sophistication of the people of these periods. The development of styles can be followed through the decoration of metal objects and ceramics, while a more distinct pictorial art is found in the rock art from many parts of Europe, in the wall paintings from Minoan Crete, and in the odd figures and scenarios engraved on a range of materials. Stylistic developments show the existence of workshops and schools, and the degree of influence they exercised reached into far corners of the Bronze and Iron Age communities. In the stylistic development during the Metal Ages, two phenomena are of particular interest. The first is the development of the sun-bird-ship motif of the Urnfield culture. The origin of this motif, which featured bird-headed ships embellished with solar disks, is not known, but over a short period about 1400 BC it became common both as incised decoration and as plastic

A prehistoric rock carving discovered in Sweden. The image is reminiscent of the sun-bird-ship motif made popular in prehistoric Europe by the Bronze Age Urnfield culture. M. Seemuller/De Agostini Picture Library/Getty Images

art throughout a vast area of eastern and central Europe. The similarity in execution and composition is remarkable and suggests a shared understanding of its meaning and the intensity of contact between distant areas.

The second point of interest is the change in style between the Hallstatt and La Tène periods. Throughout the Bronze Age and the Late Hallstatt Period, there were two distinct types of decoration in temperate Europe: the dominant geometric design of various compositions, including curvilinear styles, and the less common naturalistic style portraying humans and animals and used, for example, in rock art. At the end of the Hallstatt Period, at the beginning of the second phase of the Iron Age, a new decorative style, the La Tène style developed, and it rapidly replaced the geometric decoration. This style, as abstract as the Bronze Age one, was nonetheless substantially different. It incorporated flowing curved lines of floral designs with zoomorphic motifs filling the surfaces of the objects and increasingly used settings of semiprecious stones and coral. During the Iron Age this style flourished and branched out into different schools of great beauty. The style reached its mature form in the 4th century BC with the Waldalgesheim style, and, after this point, its most interesting branch was found in Britain, which saw a very individual development and where La Tène art continued to flourish after this style had passed its zenith on the Continent. The La Tène style was used on a variety of artifacts, such as gold and silver jewelry, swords and scabbards, shields inlaid with enamel, bronze mirrors, and beautifully executed containers in wood and ceramics.

The origin and spread of the different art styles have been the subject of much debate. Early Bronze Age geometric and linear motifs, in particular the use of double-axe and spirals motifs, looked to be the result of Mycenaean influences. The art of the Urnfield culture was thought to be the result of an invasion of people from the east, bringing cremation and a new art style into Europe. La Tène art was associated with the Celtic people, and their spread throughout large parts of Europe was assumed to have brought this art to different areas. The genesis of the various artistic developments cannot easily be established, but they were not as unified a phenomenon as has been assumed, and local variations are prolific. Different art styles influenced each other and were spread widely through copies, exchange, and communication, but this was interspersed with periods of greater local diversity and less desire for contact and emulation.

THE PEOPLE OF THE METAL AGES

The Iron Age is often seen as the time of the appearance in history of the European peoples, the "barbarians" as they were seen by Rome. These people included a number of different tribes and groups, the configuration of which changed over time. All had more or less obvious roots in the Bronze Age. Ethnicity is not easy to establish, however, and the fact that, for example, the Romans ascribed an area to a particular people does not necessarily mean that those inhabiting that area constituted an ethnic and linguistic group. Continuous changes in the composition of tribal formation occurred in the Iron Age as groups bound together through alliances created by gift giving, trade, and aggression. From Greek, and later Roman, writers and from Assyrian texts, historical information about some of these people has been preserved. The main groups presented by these texts are the Celts in western Europe, the Germanic people of northern Europe, the Slavs from eastern Europe, and Cimmerians, Scythians, and, later, Sarmatians coming into southeastern Europe from the Russian Steppe. The texts describe what to their authors appeared as barbarous customs in cultures they did not understand, but they also provide historic insights into the movements of different peoples and tribes during this unrestful period.

It was also during the Iron Age that individually named people appeared for the first time in European sources, and the names of kings, heroes, gods, and goddesses have become known through legendary writers such as Homer. In the main, however, the Metal Ages were before literature began to immortalize individuals, and in general little is known about individual people or even groups from these periods. It remains up to the archaeologist to explain how the people lived and who they were, since they are known only through their art, their actions, and their own physical remains. Their art shows the people through figures and drawings, but always in a stylistic or symbolic way rather than as portraits. This is even the case in the wall paintings from Mycenaean Crete, which show detailed full-figure drawings of women and men in different costumes and involved in various, presumably partly ceremonial, activities. The figurative representations, whether drawings or statues, do not give accurate insight into the appearance, health, and mentality of these people, but evidence of this is provided by their physical remains and the things they made and used.

Their appearance can to some extent be reconstructed on the basis of skeletal materials from graves. Owing to changes in burial rites, these are better preserved from some periods than others, but in general there is good evidence. The people were close to the same height as people living today and were of a similar build. In some areas, as demonstrated by the Early Bronze Age cemetery at Ripa Lui Bodai, in Romania, people of different racial characteristics were buried in a similar manner within one cemetery, suggesting that the population was racially mixed. It is quite likely that such mixture was common in many areas, suggesting that the cultures correspond to social structures rather than ethnic or racial ones.

The mortality rate was high, and the average life expectancy was about 30–40 years, with high infant mortality and few very old members of society. At the Unetician cemetery at Tornice, Pol., the average age at death for men was 31 and for women 20, while that from the Early Bronze Age cemetery at Lerna, Greece, was 31–37 for men and 29–31 for women. Women would have given birth at an early age, and their lower life expectancy was likely due to death in connection with pregnancy or childbirth. The difference in life expectancy may be indirect evidence of girl-child infanticide. Generational time would have been short, and the nature of society was therefore drastically different. As an example, the estimate of the living population at Branč suggests that it consisted of 30 to 40 people, half of them children. This would have influenced social life, kinship systems, and subsistence activities. The bodies often show signs of heavy physical labour, and the wear on the bones suggests that many activities took place in a squatting position.

Generally, social divisions of labour and resources did not in the Bronze Age reach such degrees that this affected the bodies, but this changed with time. Analysis of the human bones from the Early Iron Age cemetery at Mount Magdalenska, Slovenia, shows such divisions. The males of some clans or leading families had more access to animal products than any of the other members of the community, and the women generally had a more restricted and homogeneous diet. With the advent of the Iron Age, the society had become so differentiated that some people lived a life protected from hard labour and physical toils while others worked extensively and had a poor diet.

Throughout the Metal Ages, humans were victims of various diseases, such as rheumatism and arthritis, which complicated life and crippled the body. Tuberculosis also has been observed, as have periodontal disease, caries, and bone tumours. Some of these diseases caused joint changes or vertebral deformities—such as were seen on a Copper Age skeleton found in Hungary—which resulted in restricted working and even walking capacities for the individual concerned. Badly crippled and handicapped people often survived, and they must have been taken care of and fed by other members of their community.

There is also evidence to suggest that people took great care with their appearance. The hairstyles were often sophisticated, with braids, hairnets, and ornaments being used by women or with the hair cut straight at the shoulder in a bob as for the girl in the grave at Egtved, Den. Manicure equipment was common in Late Bronze and Early Iron Age graves, and the mirror was a favoured object among both the Celtic people and Scythian warriors. These objects and evidence from well-preserved graves show people as well-groomed individuals who shaved regularly, braided or cut their hair, and had well-cared-for, manicured hands.

In addition to how the people looked, there is also evidence of the clothing and ornaments they used. There are a few scattered wool textiles from the Neolithic, but the first well-documented evidence of wool textiles dates from the Bronze Age. At times the textiles themselves have been found, but more commonly it is the equipment used in textile production that shows their presence. Spindle whorls, loom weights, and combs became increasingly common components of settlement debris, showing weaving as a household task performed at any settlement. With the Iron Age, new weaving techniques developed, and embroideries, dyes, and more complicated designs were introduced, as were textiles of materials such as linen and silk. At this point, it also became common to have specialist weavers, and in some oppida the weavers lived in certain designated quarters within the settlement. The increase in textile production meant that the raising of sheep intensified in many regions during the Bronze Age. In the Aegean, this happened early in the Bronze Age, and tablets that give accounts of trade in textiles certify the economic importance of this commodity for this area. In other parts of Europe, it took a little longer, but, toward the end of the Bronze Age, changes in the fleece of sheep in England demonstrate how substantially the use of sheep had grown.

Remains of Bronze Age costumes are limited, but they show various relatively simple wool garments adorned with bronze ornaments and attachments. In many areas, hats of different kinds—possibly with a clear distinction in style between those worn by men and women—were used. Bronze statues show similarly prominent headpieces, and they often gave great attention to depicting hairstyles. In the course of the Early Bronze Age, pins became common elements of costumes, and with the Tumulus culture they became prominent pieces, at times exceeding 12 to 16 inches (30 to 40 cm) in length, with elaborate heads that often reflect regional patterns. At this time, the pins lost much of their original functional role and became primarily display items. Their regional diversity suggests how people used elements of their dress to express their group identity. During the Late Bronze Age, the pin remained in use and of importance. Thousands were found in the Swiss lake sites, but these are small elegant pieces that at times were composed into complex breast pieces by connecting chains and pendants. Iron Age textiles are found much more frequently, and clothing at that time became an elaborate and colourful medium of regional and social variability. Metal attachments became less common; but the fibula (a brooch resembling a safety pin) replaced the pin, and it became an object of fashion widely adopted and undergoing much regional development and elaboration.

These were the people who lived with and created the Metal Ages of prehistoric Europe. The conditions of their lives had undergone considerable changes during the centuries of the Copper, Bronze, and Iron ages, but these were gradual changes initiated and managed largely internally and at a rate dictated from within. Roman expansion into temperate Europe during the last centuries BC changed this, and new social and ideological structures were imposed from above upon local communities. Long-established links of contact and previous cultural affinities were broken, and a new Europe came into being.

CHAPTER 3

GREEKS, ROMANS, AND BARBARIANS

The first European civilizations—sophisticated cultures noted for their use of writing, their construction of cities, and their establishment of complex social, economic, and political structures—developed in the area of the Aegean Sea. The flowering of the ancient Greek civilizations marks the beginning of the so-called Classical period of European history, also known as Classical antiquity, which encompasses the eras dominated by the ancient Greeks and their successors, the ancient Romans. The empire of ancient Rome, in turn, was eclipsed by migrating and invading Germanic peoples, known as "barbarians" to the Romans. This chapter provides a brief cultural overview of the ancient Greeks, Romans, and barbarians, outlining their profound influence on European history.

GREEKS

Of the Indo-European tribes of European origin, the Greeks were foremost with respect to both the period at which they developed an advanced culture and their importance in further evolution. The Greeks emerged in the course of the 2nd millennium BC through the superimposition of a branch of the Indo-Europeans on the population of the Mediterranean region during the great migrations of nations that started in the region of the lower Danube. From 1800 BC onward the first early Greeks reached their later areas of settlement between the Ionian and the Aegean seas. The fusion of these earliest

Greek-speaking people with their predecessors produced the civilization known as Mycenaean. They penetrated to the sea into the Aegean region and via Crete (approximately 1400 BC) reached Rhodes and even Cyprus and the shores of Anatolia. From 1200 BC onward the Dorians followed from Epirus. They occupied principally parts of the Peloponnese (Sparta and Argolis) and also Crete. Their migration was followed by the Dark Ages—two centuries of chaotic movements of tribes in Greece—at the end of which (*c.* 900 BC) the distribution of the Greek mainland among the various tribes was on the whole completed.

From about 800 BC there was a further Greek expansion through the founding of colonies overseas. The coasts and islands of Anatolia were occupied from south to north by the Dorians, Ionians, and Aeolians, respectively. In addition, individual colonies were strung out around the shores of the Black Sea in the north and across the eastern Mediterranean to Naukratis on the Nile delta and in Cyrenaica and also in the western Mediterranean in Sicily, lower Italy, and Massalia (Marseille). Thus, the Hellenes, as they called themselves thereafter, came into contact on all sides with the old, advanced cultures of the Middle East and transmitted many features of these cultures to western Europe. This, along with the Greeks' own achievements, laid the foundations of European civilization.

A Nation of City-States

The position and nature of the country exercised a decisive influence in the evolution of Greek civilization. The proximity of the sea tempted the Greeks to range far and wide exploring it, but the fact of their living on islands or on peninsulas or in valleys separated by mountains on the mainland confined the formation of states to small areas not easily accessible from other parts. This fateful

individualism in political development was also a reflec-
tion of the Hellenic temperament. Though it prevented
Greece from becoming a single unified nation that could
rival the strength of the Middle Eastern monarchies, it led
to the evolution of the city-state. This was not merely a
complex social and economic structure and a centre for
crafts and for trade with distant regions; above all it was a
tightly knit, self-governing political and religious community whose citizens were prepared to make any sacrifice
to maintain their freedom. Colonies, too, started from
individual cities and took the form of independent city-
states. Fusions of power occurred in the shape of leagues
of cities, such as the Peloponnesian League, the Delian
League, and the Boeotian League. The efficacy of these
leagues depended chiefly upon the hegemony of a leading
city (Sparta, Athens, or Thebes), but the desire for self-
determination of the others could never be permanently
suppressed, and the leagues broke up again and again.

PEOPLE OF ACHIEVEMENT

The Hellenes, however, always felt themselves to be
one people. They were conscious of a common character and a common language, and they practiced only one
religion. Furthermore, the great athletic contests and
artistic competitions had a continually renewed unifying
effect. The Hellenes possessed a keen intellect, capable
of abstraction, and at the same time a supple imagination. They developed, in the form of the belief in the
unity of body and soul, a serene, sensuous conception of
the world. Their gods were connected only loosely by a
theogony that took shape gradually. In the Greek religion there was neither revelation nor dogma to oppose
the spirit of inquiry.

Figures engaged in the ancient Olympic Games, as depicted on a Greek vase.
Hulton Archive/Getty Images

The Hellenes benefited greatly from the knowledge and achievement of other countries in the fields of astronomy, chronology, and mathematics, but it was through their own native abilities that they made their greatest achievements, in becoming the founders of European philosophy and science. Their achievement in representative art and in architecture was no less fundamental. Their striving for an ideal, naturalistic rendering found its fulfillment in the representation of the human body in sculpture in the round. Another considerable achievement was the development of the pillared temple to a greater degree of harmony. In poetry the genius of the Hellenes created both form and content, which have remained a constant source of inspiration in European literature.

POLITICAL DEVELOPMENTS

The strong political sense of the Greeks produced a variety of systems of government from which their theory of political science abstracted types of constitution that are still in use. On the whole, political development in Greece followed a pattern: first the rule of kings, found as early as the period of Mycenaean civilization; then a feudal period, the oligarchy of noble landowners; and, finally, varying degrees of democracy. Frequently there were periods when individuals seized power in the cities and ruled as tyrants. The tendency for ever-wider sections of the community to participate in the life of the state brought into being the free democratic citizens, but the institution of slavery, upon which Greek society and the Greek economy rested, was untouched by this.

In spite of continual internal disputes, the Greeks succeeded in warding off the threat of Asian despotism. The advance of the Persians into Europe failed (490 and 480–79 BC) because of the resistance of the Greeks and in particular of the Athenians. The 5th century BC saw the highest development of Greek civilization. The Classical period of Athens and its great accomplishments left a lasting impression, but the political cleavages, particularly the struggle between Athens and Sparta, increasingly reduced the political strength of the Greeks.

GREEK INFLUENCE

Not until they were conquered by the Macedonians in the 4th century BC did the Greeks attain a new importance as the cultural leaven of the so-called Hellenistic empires of the Macedonian king Alexander the Great and his successors. A new system of colonization spread as far as the Indus city-communities fashioned after the Greek

The ancient city of Athens as it appeared in the 2nd century AD. At its peak in the 5th century BC, Athens was the birthplace of unparalleled intellectual and artistic achievement. Archive Photos/Getty Images

prototype, and Greek education and language came to be of consequence in the world at large.

Greece again asserted its independence through the formation of the Achaean League, which was finally defeated by the Romans in 146 BC. The spirit of Greek civilization subsequently exercised a great influence upon Rome. Greek culture became one of the principal components of Roman imperial culture and together with it spread throughout Europe. When Christian teaching appeared in the Middle East, the Greek world of ideas exercised a decisive influence upon its spiritual evolution. From the time of the partition of the Roman Empire, leadership in the Eastern Empire fell to the Greeks. Their language became the language of the state, and its usage spread to the Balkans. The Byzantine Empire, of which Greece was the core, protected Europe against potential

Achaean League

The Achaean League was a 3rd-century-BC confederation of the towns of Achaea in ancient Greece. The 12 Achaean cities of the northern Peloponnese had organized a league by the 4th century BC to protect themselves against piratical raids from across the Corinthian Gulf, but this league fell apart after the death of Alexander the Great. The 10 surviving cities renewed their alliance in 280 BC, and under the leadership of Aratus of Sicyon, the league gained strength by the inclusion of his city, and later other non-Achaean cities, on equal terms.

At the head of the Achaean League were two generals (*strategoi*) until a single general was substituted in 255 BC. The general was the annually elected head of the league's army, and a particular general could not be immediately reelected. The general headed the league's administrative board, whose 10 members in turn presided over the various city-states' representative councils and assemblies. These bodies of citizenry could vote on matters submitted to them by the general. The minimum voting age in the assemblies was 30 years of age.

Under the Achaean League's federal constitution, its city-state members had almost complete autonomy within the framework of the league's central administration; only matters of foreign policy, war, and federal taxes were referred to the general and the board for decision making.

invaders from Anatolia until the fall of Constantinople (the capital of the Byzantine Empire) in 1453.

ROMANS

The original Mediterranean population of Italy was completely altered by repeated superimpositions of peoples of Indo-European stock. The first Indo-European migrants, who belonged to the Italic tribes, moved across the eastern Alpine passes into the plain of the Po River about 1800 BC. Later they crossed the Apennines and eventually occupied the region of Latium, which included Rome. Before 1000 BC there followed related tribes, which later divided into various groups and gradually moved to central and southern Italy. In Tuscany they were repulsed by the Etruscans, who may have come originally from Anatolia. The next to arrive were Illyrians from the Balkans, who occupied Venetia and Apulia. At the beginning of the historical period, Greek colonists arrived in Italy, and after 400 BC the Celts settled in the plain of the Po.

The city of Rome, increasing gradually in power and influence, created through political rule and the spread of the Latin language something like a nation out of this abundance of nationalities. In this the Romans were favoured by their kinship with the other Italic tribes. The Roman and Italic elements in Italy, moreover, were reinforced in the beginning through the founding of colonies by Rome and by other towns in Latium. The Italic element in Roman towns decreased through a process—less racial than cultural—called the Romanization of the provinces. In the 3rd century BC, central and southern Italy were dotted with Roman colonies, and the system was to be extended to ever more distant regions up to imperial times. As its dominion spread throughout Italy and covered the entire Mediterranean basin, Rome received an influx of people of the most varied origins, including eventually vast numbers from Asia and Africa.

THE ROMAN EMPIRE

The building of an enormous empire was Rome's greatest achievement. Held together by the military power of one city, in the 2nd century AD the Roman Empire extended throughout northern Africa and western Asia; in Europe it covered all the Mediterranean countries, Spain, Gaul, and southern Britain. This vast region, united under a single authority and a single political and social organization, enjoyed a long period of peaceful development. In Asia, on a narrow front, it bordered the Parthian empire, but elsewhere beyond its perimeter there were only barbarians. Rome brought to the conquered parts of Europe the civilization the Greeks had begun, to which it added its own important contributions in the form of state organization, military institutions, and law.

Within the framework of the empire and under the protection of its chain of fortifications, extending uninterrupted the entire length of its frontiers (marked in Europe by the Rhine and the Danube), there began the assimilation of varying types of culture to the Hellenistic-Roman pattern. The army principally, but also Roman administration, the social order, and economic factors, encouraged Romanization. Except around the eastern Mediterranean, where Greek remained dominant, Latin

Roman legions—military units comprising several thousand men—kept the peace and encouraged unity within the Roman Empire. Rob Shone/ Getty Images

became everywhere the language of commerce and eventually almost the universal language.

ROMAN GOVERNMENT AND CITIZENRY

The empire formed an interconnected area of free trade, which was afforded a thriving existence by the *pax romana* ("Roman peace"). Products of rural districts found a market throughout the whole empire, and the advanced technical skills of the central region of the Mediterranean spread outward into the provinces. The most decisive step toward Romanization was the extension of the city system into these provinces. Rural and tribal institutions were replaced by the *civitas* form of government, according to which the elected city authority shared in the administration of the surrounding country region, and, as the old idea of the Greek city-state gained ground, a measure of local autonomy appeared. The Romanized upper classes of the provinces began supplying men to fill the higher offices of the state. Ever-larger numbers of people acquired the status of Roman citizens, until in AD 212 the emperor Caracalla bestowed it on all freeborn subjects. The institution of slavery, however, remained.

The enjoyment of equal rights by all Roman citizens did not last. The coercive measures by which alone the state could maintain itself divided the population anew into hereditary classes according to their work. The barbarians, mainly Germanic, who were admitted into the empire in greater numbers, remained in their own tribal associations either as subjects or as allies. The state created a perfected administrative apparatus, which exercised a strongly unifying effect throughout the empire, but local self-government became less and less effective under pressure from the central authority.

THE EMPIRE'S DECLINE

The decline of the late empire was accompanied by a stagnation of spiritual forces, a paralysis of creative power, and a retrograde development in the economy. Much of the empire's work of civilization was lost in internal and external wars. Equally, barbarization began with the rise of unchecked pagan ways of life and the settlement of Germanic tribes long before the latter shattered the Western Empire and took possession of its parts. Though many features of Roman civilization disappeared, others survived in the customs of peoples in various parts of the empire. Moreover, something of the superstructure of the empire was taken over by the Germanic states, and much valuable literature was preserved in manuscript for later times.

ROME AND CHRISTIANITY

It was under the Roman Empire that the Christian religion penetrated into Europe. By winning recognition as the religion of the state, it added a new basic factor of equality and unification to the imperial civilization and at the same time reintroduced Middle Eastern and Hellenistic elements into the West. Organized within the framework of the empire, the church became a complementary body upholding the state. Moreover, during the period of the decline of secular culture, Christianity and the church were the sole forces to arouse fresh creative strength by assimilating the civilization of the ancient world and transmitting it to the Middle Ages.

At the same time, the church in the West showed reserve toward the speculative dogma of the Middle Eastern and Hellenic worlds and directed its attention more toward questions of morality and order. When the Western Empire collapsed and the use of Greek had died

Shepherd mural from the Roman catacombs of Saint-Callixtus. As the offi-cially recognized religion of the Roman Empire, Christianity soon flourished throughout Europe. Roger Viollet/Getty Images

there, the division between East and West became still sharper. The name Romaioi remained attached to the Greeks of the Eastern Empire, while in the West the word Roman developed a new meaning in connection with the church and the bishop of Rome. Christianity and a church of a Roman character, the most enduring legacy of the ancient world, became one of the most important features in western European civilization.

BARBARIAN MIGRATIONS AND INVASIONS

The wanderings of the Germanic peoples, which lasted until the early Middle Ages and destroyed the Western Roman Empire, were, together with the migrations of the Slavs, formative elements of the distribution of peoples in modern Europe. The Germanic peoples originated about 1800 BC from the superimposition of Battle-Ax people from the Corded Ware culture of middle Germany on a population of megalithic culture on the eastern North Sea coast. During the Bronze Age the Germanic peoples spread over southern Scandinavia and penetrated more deeply into Germany between the Weser and Vistula rivers. Contact with the Mediterranean through the amber trade encouraged the development from a purely peasant culture, but during the Iron Age the Germanic peoples were at first cut off from the Mediterranean by the Celts and Illyrians. Their culture declined, and an increasing population, together with worsening climatic conditions, drove them to seek new lands farther south. Thus the central European Celts and Illyrians found themselves under a growing pressure. Even before 200 BC the first Germanic tribes had reached the lower Danube, where their path was barred by the Macedonian kingdom. Driven by rising floodwaters, at the end of the 2nd century BC, migratory hordes of Cimbri, Teutoni, and Ambrones from Jutland broke through the Celtic-Illyrian zone and reached the edge of the Roman sphere of influence, appearing first in Carinthia (113 BC), then in southern France, and finally in upper Italy. With the violent attacks of the Cimbri, the Germans stepped onto the stage of history.

THE GERMANS AND HUNS

The migrations of the Germanic peoples were in no way nomadic; they were the gradual expansions of a land-hungry peasantry. Tribes did not always migrate en masse. Usually, because of the loose political structure, groups remained in the original homelands or settled down at points along the migration route. In the course of time, many tribes were depleted and scattered. On the other hand, different tribal groups would sometimes unite before migrating or would take up other wanderers en route. The migrations required skilled leadership, and this promoted the social and political elevation of a noble and kingly class.

In 102 BC the Teutoni were totally defeated by the Romans, who in the following year destroyed the army of the Cimbri. The Swabian tribes, however, moved steadily through central and southern Germany, and the Celts were compelled to retreat to Gaul. When the Germans under Ariovistus crossed the upper Rhine, Julius Caesar arrested their advance and initiated the Roman counter-movement with his victory in the Sundgau (58 BC). Under the emperor Augustus, Roman rule was carried as far as the Rhine and the Danube. On the far side of these rivers, the Germans were pushed back only in the small area contained within the Germano-Raetian limes (fortified frontier) from about AD 70.

The pressure of population was soon evident once more among the German peoples. Tribes that had left

Scandinavia earlier (Rugii, Goths, Gepidae, Vandals, Burgundians, and others) pressed on from the lower Vistula and Oder rivers (AD 150 onward). The unrest spread to other tribes, and the resulting wars between the Romans and the Marcomanni (166–180) threatened Italy itself. The successful campaigns of Marcus Aurelius resulted in the acquisition by Rome of the provinces of Marcomannia and Sarmatia, but after his death these had to be abandoned and the movement of the Germanic peoples continued. Soon the Alemanni, pushing up the Main River, reached the upper German limes.

To the east the Goths had reached the Black Sea about AD 200. Year after year Goths and others, either crossing the lower Danube or traveling by sea, penetrated into the Balkan Peninsula and Anatolia as far as Cyprus on plundering expeditions. Only with the Roman victory at Naissus (269) was their advance finally checked. Enriched with booty and constituted imperial mercenaries in return for the payment of a yearly tribute, they became a settled population. The Romans, however, surrendered Dacia beyond the Danube.

In 258 the Alemanni and the Franks broke through the lines and settled on the right bank of the Rhine, continuously infiltrating thereafter toward Gaul and Italy. Everywhere within the empire, towns were fortified, even Rome itself. Franks and Saxons ravaged the coasts of northern Gaul and Britain, and for the next three centuries incursions by Germanic peoples were the scourge of the Western Empire. Nevertheless, it was only with German help that the empire was able to survive as long as it did. The Roman army received an ever-growing number of recruits from the German tribes, which also provided settlers for the land. The Germans soon proved themselves capable of holding the highest ranks in the army.

Tribute money to the tribes, pay to individual soldiers, and booty all brought wealth to the Germans, which in turn gave warrior lords the means with which to maintain large followings of retainers.

In the West, however, among the Alemanni and Franks, the beginnings of political union into larger groups did not go beyond loose associations. Only in the East did the Gothic kingdom gather many tribes under a single leadership. Above all, the development of the eastern Germans was stimulated by their undisturbed contact with the frontiers of the ancient world. Their economy, however, was still unable to support the needs of a steadily growing population, and pressure from overpopulation resulted in further incursions into the Roman Empire. The imperial reforms of Diocletian and Constantine the Great brought a period of improvement. The usurpation of the imperial title by a Frankish general in 356 let loose a storm along the length of the Rhine and subsequently on the Danube, but the frontiers were restored by the forces of the emperors Julian and Valentinian I, who repelled attacks by both the Franks and the Alemanni.

At that time, a new force appeared. In 375 the Huns from Central Asia first attacked the Ostrogoths—an event that provoked serious disturbances among the eastern Germans. The Huns remained in the background, gradually subjugating many Germanic and other tribes. The terrified Goths and related tribes burst through the Danube frontier into the Roman Empire, and the Balkans became once again a battlefield for German armies. After the crushing defeat of the Romans at Adrianople (378), the empire was no longer in a position to drive all its enemies from its territories. Tribes that could no longer be expelled were settled within the empire as "allies" (*foederati*). They received subsidies and in return supplied

Portrait of Attila the Hun. Hulton Archive/Getty Images

troops. The Germanization of the empire progressed, that of the army being nearly completed. None of the tribes, however, that had broken into the Balkans settled there. After the division of the empire in 395, the emperors at Constantinople did all in their power to drive the Germanic tribes away from the vicinity of the capital toward the Western Empire.

From the beginning of the 5th century, the Western Empire was the scene of numerous further migrations. The Visigoths broke out of the Balkans into Italy and in 410 temporarily occupied Rome. In 406–407, Germanic and other tribes (Vandals, Alani, Suebi, and Burgundians) from Silesia and even farther east crossed the Rhine in their flight from the Huns and penetrated as far as Spain. The Vandals subsequently crossed to Africa and set up at Carthage the first independent German state on Roman soil. In the Battle of the Catalaunian Plains (451), the Roman commander Aëtius, with German support, defeated Attila, who had united his Huns with some other Germans in a vigorous westward push. The Balkans suffered a third period of terrible raids from the eastern Germans; and Jutes, Angles, and Saxons from the Jutland Peninsula crossed over to Britain. The Franks and the Alemanni finally established themselves on the far side of the Rhine, the Burgundians extended along the Rhône valley, and the Visigoths took possession of nearly all of Spain. In 476 the Germanic soldiery proclaimed Odoacer, a barbarian general, as king of Italy, and, when Odoacer deposed the emperor Romulus Augustulus at Ravenna, the empire in the West was at an end. In the East, imperial rule remained a reality, and Constantinople, also called "New Rome," survived many sieges until its fall in 1453. In comparison, "Old Rome" declined into an episcopal centre, losing many of its imperial characteristics.

An illustration depicting Roman emperor Romulus Augustulus relinquishing the crown to the conquering barbarian general Odoacer. Bob Thomas/Popperfoto/Getty Images

THE RECONFIGURATION OF THE EMPIRE

By the end of the 5th century, most of the non-Roman peoples settled in the West were adopting Roman customs and Christian belief. Intermarriage with established Roman families, the assumption of imperial titles, and, finally, conversion assisted a process of acculturation among their leaders, for instance, in the case of Clovis, the Frank. Theodoric the Ostrogoth established an impressive "sub-Roman" kingdom based on Ravenna, where public buildings and churches served by an Arian clergy competed with imperial monuments. Increased Roman influence can also be seen in the law codes promulgated by the Visigoths Euric (late 5th century) and Alaric II (the Breviary of 506) and the Burgundians, Bavarians, Ostrogoths, and Franks (Lex Salica, 507–511). Christianity often provided the medium for incorporation into old imperial structures. While the Goths were still in the Danube basin, they had embraced Arian Christianity (which denied that the Son was of the same substance as the Father), and their first bishop, Ulfilas, translated the Bible into Gothic. Given its heretical nature, this religious literature in a written vernacular could not survive, and, with conversion to orthodox ("catholic") Christianity, the barbarian languages gradually gave way to Latin.

Nonetheless, the Germanic tribes brought into Europe their own tribal institutions, ethnic patterns, and oral and artistic traditions, including a highly developed epic poetry. Their influence was strongest in central Europe, where the Romans had had the least impact; less marked in the northern and eastern parts, where Romano-British and Gallo-Roman cultures were established; and weakest in the highly Romanized southern regions. Linguistically, Old High German developed in the first zone and Anglo-Saxon in Britain, while farther south medieval Romance languages developed from their common Latin inheritance.

In the southern zone, imperial traditions were reinforced by the reconquest, albeit brief, of North Africa, Italy, and parts of Spain by forces from Constantinople under Justinian's general Belisarius. Despite the restoration of Roman administration between 533 and 554 (celebrated in the mosaics of Ravenna and the Pragmatic Sanction of 554), imperial forces could not prevent the Lombards from moving inexorably into northern Italy, which they occupied in 568. The reconquered parts of the Western Empire were thus reduced to a narrow strip of territory from the head of the Adriatic to Ravenna, the exarchate, Rome—now governed effectively by its bishop—plus small duchies. In addition, Sicily, Bruttium, and Calabria remained subject to Constantinople and were Greek-speaking for many centuries.

In contrast to previous invaders, from the 6th century onward, newly arrived barbarian forces clung to their pagan culture and resisted assimilation. The Saxons established themselves east of the Rhine in the north. The Avars and their Slav allies, who moved steadily westward from the Vistula and Dnieper river basins, disrupted weak imperial defenses at the Danube and pressed south and west into the Balkans and central Europe. By 567 the Avars established control over the Hungarian plain, where they remained until their defeat by Charlemagne in 796. After successfully besieging Sirmium and Singidunum in the 580s, the eastern Slavs infiltrated the Balkans, while others moved north and west to settle eventually along the Elbe beside the Saxons. The failure of the combined Avaro-Slav siege of Constantinople in 626 ended this pagan expansion. Although Slavs occupied the Balkan Peninsula for two centuries or more, disrupting east-west communication along the ancient Via Egnatia, they were eventually evangelized and absorbed into the Eastern Empire.

THE MIDDLE AGES

The period of European history extending from about AD 500 to 1400–1500 is traditionally known as the Middle Ages. Although once regarded as a time of uninterrupted ignorance, superstition, and social oppression, the Middle Ages are now understood as a dynamic period during which the idea of Europe as a distinct cultural unit emerged.

During late antiquity and the early Middle Ages, political, social, economic, and cultural structures were profoundly reorganized, as Roman imperial traditions gave way to those of the Germanic peoples who established kingdoms in the former Western Empire. New forms of political leadership were introduced, the population of Europe was gradually Christianized, and monasticism was established as the ideal form of religious life. These developments reached their mature form in the 9th century during the reign of Charlemagne and other rulers of the Carolingian dynasty, who oversaw a broad cultural revival known as the Carolingian Renaissance.

In the central, or high, Middle Ages, even more dramatic growth occurred. The period was marked by economic and territorial expansion, demographic and urban growth, the emergence of national identity, and the restructuring of secular and ecclesiastical institutions. It was the era of the Crusades, Gothic art and architecture, the papal monarchy, the birth of the university, the recovery of ancient Greek thought, and the soaring intellectual achievements of St. Thomas Aquinas (c. 1224–74).

It has been traditionally held that by the 14th century the dynamic force of medieval civilization had been

Calendar illustration for April from the Très Riches Heures du duc de Berry, *manuscript illuminated by the Limbourg brothers, 1416.* Photos. com/Jupiterimages

spent and that the late Middle Ages were characterized by decline and decay. Europe did indeed suffer disasters of war, famine, and pestilence in the 14th century, but many of the underlying social, intellectual, and political structures remained intact. In the 15th and 16th centuries, Europe experienced an intellectual and economic revival, conventionally called the Renaissance, that laid the foundation for the subsequent expansion of European culture throughout the world.

Many historians have questioned the conventional dating of the beginning and end of the Middle Ages, which were never precise in any case and cannot be located in any year or even century. Some scholars have advocated extending the period defined as late antiquity (*c.* 250–*c.* 750) into the 10th century or later, and some have proposed a Middle Ages lasting from about 1000 to 1800. Still others argue for the inclusion of the old periods Middle Ages, Renaissance, and Reformation into a single period beginning in late antiquity and ending in the second half of the 16th century.

THE IDEA OF THE MIDDLE AGES

The term Middle Ages was first used by 15th-century scholars to designate the period between their own time and the fall of the Western Roman Empire. Although it remains both a commonplace colloquial term and the name of a subject of academic study, there has been much scholarly debate about its appropriateness. Both the history of the term and the debate over its use are reminders that historical periods are cultural and social constructs, based on later perceptions of the past, and that human life often changes quite rapidly within labeled periods, however designated.

THE TERM AND CONCEPT BEFORE
THE 18TH CENTURY

From the 4th to the 15th century, writers of history
thought within a linear framework of time derived from
the Christian understanding of Scripture—the sequence
of Creation, Incarnation, Christ's Second Coming, and
the Last Judgment. In Book XXII of *City of God*, the
great Church Father Augustine of Hippo (354–430) pos-
ited six ages of world history, which paralleled the six days
of Creation and the six ages of the individual human life
span. For Augustine, the six ages of history—from Adam
and Eve to the Flood, from the Flood to Abraham, from
Abraham to King David, from David to the Babylonian
Exile, from the Exile to Jesus Christ, and from Christ to
the Second Coming—would be followed by a seventh
age, the reign of Christ on earth. World history was conceived as "salvation history"—the course of events from
Creation to the Last Judgment—and its purposes were
religious and moral. Thus, all the references by Augustine
and other early authors to a "middle time" must be understood within the framework of the sixth age of salvation
history. Early Christian interpretations of the biblical
Book of Daniel (Daniel 2:31–45, 7), especially those of the
Church Father Jerome (*c.* 347–419/420) and the historian
Paulus Orosius (flourished 414–417), added the idea of
four successive world empires—Babylon, Persia, Greece,
and Rome. Late writers in this tradition added the idea
of the *translation imperii* ("translation of empire"): from
Alexander the Great to the Romans, from the Romans
to the Franks under Charlemagne in 800, and from
Charlemagne to the East Frankish emperors and Otto I. A
number of early European thinkers built upon the idea of
the translation of empire to define European civilization
in terms of scholarship and chivalry (the knightly code of

conduct). All these ideas were readily compatible with the Augustinian sequence of the six ages of the world.

The single exception to this trend was the work of the late 12th-century Calabrian abbot and scriptural exegete Joachim of Fiore (*c.* 1130– *c.* 1201). According to Joachim, there were three ages in human history: that of the Father (before Christ), that of the Son (from Christ to an unknown future date, which some of Joachim's followers located in the late 13th century), and that of the Holy Spirit (during which all Christendom would turn into a vast church with a universal priesthood of believers). But Joachim's view was also firmly expressed in terms of salvation history. Many chroniclers and writers of histories, of course, wrote about shorter periods of time and focused their efforts on local affairs, but the great Augustinian metanarrative underlay their work too. From several confessional perspectives, this view still survives.

In the 14th century, however, the literary moralist Petrarch (1304–74), fascinated with ancient Roman history and contemptuous of the time that followed it, including his own century, divided the past into ancient and new—antiquity and recent times—and located the transition between them in the 4th century, when the Roman emperors converted to Christianity. According to Petrarch, what followed was an age of *tenebrae* ("shadows"), a "sordid middle time" with only the hope of a better age to follow. Although Petrarch's disapproval of the Christianized Roman and post-Roman world may seem irreligious, he was in fact a devout Christian; his judgment was based on aesthetic, moral, and philological criteria, not Christian ones. Petrarch's limitless admiration for Rome heralded a novel conception of the European past and established criteria for historical periodization other than those of salvation history or the history of the church, empire, cities, rulers, or noble dynasties. His followers in later centuries focused primarily on the transformation of the arts and letters, seeing a renewal of earlier Roman dignity and achievement beginning with the painter Giotto (1266/67 or 1276–1337) and with Petrarch himself and continuing into the 15th and 16th centuries.

In the early 16th century, religious critics and reformers, including both the Dutch humanist Desiderius Erasmus and the Protestant reformer Martin Luther, added another dimension to the new conception and terminology: the idea of an evangelical, apostolic Christian church that had become corrupt when it was absorbed by the Roman Empire and now needed to be reformed, or restored to its earlier apostolic authenticity. The idea of reform had long been built into the Christian worldview. This conception of the period between the 4th and 16th centuries was laid out in the great Protestant history by Matthias Flacius Illyricus, *Centuriae Magdeburgensis* (1559–74; "The Magdeburg Centuries"), which also introduced the practice of dividing the past into ostensibly neutral centuries. The Roman Catholic version of church history was reflected in the *Annales Ecclesiastici* ("Ecclesiastical Annals") of Caesar Baronius (1538–1607), completed by Oderico Rinaldi in 1677. Thus, the historical dimension of both the Protestant and the Catholic reformations of the 16th and 17th centuries added a sharply polemical religious interpretation of the Christian past to Petrarch's original conception, as church history was put to the service of confessional debate.

Petrarch's cultural successors, the literary humanists, also used variants of the expression Middle Ages. Among them was *media tempestas* ("middle time"), first used by Giovanni Andrea, bishop of Aleria, in 1469; others were *media antiquitas* ("middle antiquity"), *media aetas* ("middle era"), and *media tempora* ("middle times"), all first used between 1514 and 1530. The political theorist and historian

Melchior Goldast appears to have coined the variation *medium aevum* ("a middle age") in 1604; shortly after, in a Latin work of 1610, the English jurist and legal historian John Selden repeated *medium aevum*, Anglicizing the term in 1614 to *middle times* and in 1618 to *middle ages*. In 1641 the French historian Pierre de Marca apparently coined the French vernacular term *le moyen âge*, which gained authority in the respected lexicographical work *Glossarium ad scriptores mediae et infimae latinitatis* (1678; "A Glossary for Writers of Middle and Low Latin"), by Charles du Fresne, seigneur du Cange, who emphasized the inferior and "middle" quality of Latin linguistic usage after the 4th century. Other 17th-century historians, including Gisbertus Voetius and Georg Horn, used terms such as *media aetas* in their histories of the church before the Reformation of the 16th century.

The term and idea circulated even more widely in other historical works. Du Cange's great dictionary also used the Latin term *medium aevum*, as did the popular historical textbook *The Nucleus of Middle History Between Ancient and Modern* (1688), by the German historian Christoph Keller—although Keller observed that in naming the period he was simply following the terminology of earlier and contemporary scholars. By the late 17th century the most commonly used term for the period in Latin was *medium aevum*, and various equivalents of Middle Ages or Middle Age were used in European vernacular languages.

ENLIGHTENMENT SCORN AND ROMANTIC ADMIRATION

During the 17th and 18th centuries a number of thinkers argued that western Europe after the 15th century had surpassed even antiquity in its discoveries and technology and had thereby created a distinctively modern world.

Their views, which were sharpened by Enlightenment critics of earlier European political and religious structures, did nothing to change the image of the Middle Ages. Voltaire, in his *An Essay on Universal History, the Manners and Spirit of Nations from the Reign of Charlemaign to the Age of Lewis XIV* (1756), savaged the Latin Christian and the reformed churches for their clerical obscurantism and earlier rulers for their ruthless and arbitrary use of force. Edward Gibbon, the English historian whose great work *The Decline and Fall of the Roman Empire* (1776–88) begins with events in late antiquity and ends with the fall of Constantinople to the Ottoman Turks in 1453, categorically attributed the beginning of that very long "decline and fall" to "the triumph of barbarism and religion," thus contemptuously characterizing the entire period from the 5th to the 15th century.

But, as Gibbon's own work showed, not only had the term and the often pejorative idea of the Middle Ages been shaped in the 16th and 17th centuries, but so had the critical and technical standards of modern historical scholarship. Some Enlightenment thinkers even became interested in earlier periods of European history. Their attraction to the Middle Ages paralleled the respect for and interest in the period shared by many ideologically conservative rulers, nobles, magistrates, and churchmen. But the historians also began to apply critical techniques to their investigation of the Middle Ages. The new scholarship on the period was animated in the late 18th and early 19th centuries by historians imbued with ethnic-national sentiment and with a conception of historically "ethnic" communities—especially in Germany and England—that lacked a recognized past (or had only a peripheral past) in traditional histories of the Greco-Roman world.

During the Romantic era, an affectionate and sentimentalized portrait of the Middle Ages emerged that was usually no more accurate than the polemical characterizations of Enlightenment writers. Such views contributed to the myth that 19th-century nation-states were composed of ethnic groups that had remained unchanged and had occupied the same territory for long periods (or had once occupied territory that was now inhabited by other nation-states). These arguments became powerful and dangerous political forces in the 19th and 20th centuries, although research in the late 20th century dismissed them as political fantasies.

Not all 19th-century historians were appreciative of the Middle Ages. Although the French historian Jules Michelet at first praised the Middle Ages as the time of the birth of France, his increasing political liberalism led him to shift his admiration to the 16th century, virtually coining the term Renaissance in the process of appropriating it for France. In 1860 the Swiss historian Jacob Burckhardt published his *The Civilization of the Renaissance in Italy*, a work as widely read and influential as that of Michelet. Despite Romantic nostalgia and increasingly disciplined scholarship, the work of Michelet and Burckhardt served to fix the opposition between the Middle Ages and the Renaissance in the modern mind, generally to the disadvantage of the former. These views were sharpened by 19th-century anticlericalism, especially anti-Roman Catholicism, although they were countered by equally learned Catholic apologists.

THE MIDDLE AGES IN MODERN HISTORIOGRAPHY

With the extraordinary growth of the academic discipline of history in the 19th century, the history of the Middle Ages was absorbed into academic curricula of history in Europe and the United States and established in university survey courses and research seminars. Journals of scholarly historical research began publication in Germany (1859), France (1876), England (1886), and the United States (1895), regularly including studies of one aspect or another of the Middle Ages. Historical documents were edited and substantial scholarly literature was produced that brought the history of the Middle Ages into synchronization with other fields of history. The study of the Middle Ages developed chiefly as a part of the national histories of the individual European countries, but it was studied in the United States as a pan-European phenomenon, with a focus after World War I chiefly on English and French history. The growing influence and prestige of the new academic and professional field of medieval history were reflected in the Monumenta Germaniae Historica ("Historical Monuments of the Germans"), a research and publication institute founded in 1819 and still in existence, and in the eight-volume collaborative *Cambridge Medieval History* (1911–36). (The latter's replacement, *The New Cambridge Medieval History*, began to appear in 1998.)

Most scholars of the 19th and early 20th centuries accepted the view that history is largely a story of progress, in which occasional periods of decline—such as the Middle Ages—are succeeded by periods of renewal. The most articulate attack on this view was by the American medievalist Charles Homer Haskins in *The Renaissance of the Twelfth Century* (1927), which applied Michelet's and Burckhardt's term Renaissance to the 12th century rather than to the 15th or 16th.

Although the teaching responsibilities of academic historians of the Middle Ages still generally reflect either the original tripartite division of European history or the more recent and more common quadripartite division (ancient, medieval, early modern, and modern), most scholars specialize in only very small parts of a very long period. With the emergence of late antiquity as a distinct field of research and teaching since the mid-20th century, the early part of the conventional Middle Ages has been rethought and rewritten. The distinctive post-Classical period of late antiquity is now considered the medium through which ancient Greco-Roman traditions were passed on to later Europeans. The older image of a Classical antiquity despised by world-rejecting Christians and wiped out by savage barbarians is no longer credible.

Historians in the late 20th and early 21st centuries also debated the existence of a rapid and extensive change in European society at about the turn of the 2nd millennium. Some scholars, following the pioneering lead of the French historian Georges Duby, argued for a rapid mutation, chiefly with regard to the development of new kinds of lay and ecclesiastical power over agricultural labour and the simultaneous restructuring of aristocratic lineages in the 11th century. Others maintained that a gradual transformation of society and culture occurred over a longer period of time, beginning earlier than the 11th century. These debates influenced the concept of a long Middle Ages mentioned above.

With the emergence of the concept of early modern history, roughly from 1400 to 1800, the Middle Ages, the Renaissance, the Reformation, and the scientific revolution were subsumed into a period extending from the late 14th century to the 18th century. The creation of specialized scholarly conferences, historical journals, monograph series, and thematic collections of scholarly essays has reflected these changes in the configuration of the period.

Scholars also rethought the nature of change in different parts of Europe. They recognized the problem of the obvious differences between those European lands in late antiquity that had once been part of the Roman Empire and those that had not and therefore got their Romanism and antiquity secondhand. They also revised their understanding of the relations between the older Mediterranean world (large areas of which entered the Byzantine and Arab-Islamic cultural orbits) and northern Europe. In addition, scholars examined how Roman culture exported itself to peripheries on the north and east through a form of colonization that culminated in the absorption of originally peripheral colonies into an expanded core culture.

CHRONOLOGY

Regardless of the loaded aesthetic, philological, moral, confessional, and philosophical origins of the term Middle Ages, the period it defines is important because it witnessed the emergence of a distinctive European civilization centred in a region that was on the periphery of ancient Mediterranean civilization. Although European civilization appropriated elements of both Greco-Roman antiquity and Judeo-Christian religion and ethics, it emerged just as the ancient Mediterranean ecumenical world was divided into the civilizations of East Rome, or Byzantium, and Islam in the 7th and 8th centuries. Three sibling civilizations, two of them Christian, developed at about the same time. The influence of wider Eurasian and North African history on that of Europe has attracted the attention of increasing numbers of historians since the late 20th century. But such change does not occur in a single year and not even in a single century. To assign any but an approximate date to the beginning of the end of the Middle Ages, as was once the fashion, is pointless. Far more important is the assessment of the nature of change in different areas of life in different periods and different places between the 3rd and the 16th centuries.

The 8th-century English monk and computist Bede (673–735), adapting an invention of the 6th-century theologian Dionysius Exiguus, introduced the method of counting years from the birth of Jesus, *anno Domini* (AD; "in the year of our Lord"). The new method superseded older traditions, which included dating by four-year Olympiads, by the number of years since the founding of Rome in 753 BC, by the years of Roman consuls, by the regnal years of emperors, and by the 15-year tax assessment cycle of indictions (Roman fiscal years). Bede's innovation was taken up by Frankish chroniclers and rulers from the late 8th century and became standard practice in Europe.

The year itself was divided according to a universal Christian calendar that gradually displaced the old Roman calendar, although it retained the Roman names for the months. The liturgical year alternated seasons of penitence and joy, beginning with Advent, the fifth Sunday before Christmas, and culminating in penitential Lent and joyful Easter and its aftermath until Advent returned. Although the unit of the week and the Sabbath were taken over from Jewish usage—displacing the older Roman divisions of the month into Kalendae, Nonae, and Ides and the nine-day market cycle—Christians began to mark time by the seven-day week and moved its holiest day to Sunday during the 4th century.

LATE ANTIQUITY: THE RECONFIGURATION OF THE ROMAN WORLD

The Roman Empire of late antiquity was no longer the original empire of its founder, Augustus, nor was it even the 2nd-century entity of the emperor Marcus Aurelius. In the 3rd century the emperor, who was first called *princeps* ("first citizen") and then *dominus* ("lord"), became *divus* ("divine"). The powerful religious connotations of the imperial office were adopted even by usurpers of the imperial throne, backed by their armies, who then ruled autocratically at the head of a vast bureaucratic and military organization. Internal and external crises during the 3rd and 4th centuries resulted in the division of the empire into an eastern and a western part after 285, with the east possessing a great and flourishing capital built by the emperor Constantine—Constantinople (now Istanbul)—and far more economic, political, and military resources than the western half. The administration of the entire empire was restructured to finance immense military expenditures, giving the western European provinces and frontier areas greater importance but fewer resources. Most of the population of the empire, including soldiers, were frozen hereditarily in their occupations. The Western Empire, whose capital moved north from Rome in the 4th century to a number of provincial cities—Trier, Arles, Milan, and ultimately Ravenna—became less urbanized, more ruralized, and gradually dominated by an aristocracy of landowners and military officials, most of whom lived on large villas and in newly fortified cities. The provincial economy had become increasingly rural and localized and was dominated by the needs of the vast military bases near the frontiers.

The great and small estates were worked by slaves, freedmen, and *coloni* ("farmers"), who had once been independent but had voluntarily or involuntarily subordinated themselves to the great landowners as their only protection against imperial tax collectors or military conscription. The landowners dispensed local justice and assembled private armies, which were powerful enough to negotiate on their subordinates' behalf with imperial officials. Mediterranean trade diminished, and the production of more and more goods was undertaken locally, as was the organization of social, devotional, and political life.

Non-Roman peoples from beyond the frontiers— *barbari* ("barbarians") or *externae gentes* ("foreign peoples"), as the Romans called them—had long been allowed to enter the empire individually or in families as provincial farmers and soldiers. But after 375 a number of composite Germanic peoples, many of them only recently assembled and ruled by their own new political and military elites, entered the empire as intact groups, originally by treaty with Rome and later independently. They established themselves as rulers of a number of western provinces, particularly parts of Italy, Iberia, Gaul, and Britain, often in the name of the Roman emperor and with the cooperation of many Roman provincials.

Roman ethnography classified external peoples as distinct and ethnically homogeneous groups with unchanging identities; they were part of the order of nature. Adopting this view, philologists, anthropologists, and historians in the 19th century maintained that the Germanic "tribes" that first appeared in the 3rd century were the ethnic ancestors of the "tribes" of the 5th century and that the ethnic composition of these groups remained unchanged in the interval. Late 20th-century research in ethnogenesis thoroughly demonstrated the unreliability of Roman ethnography, although modern concepts of ethnicity continue to exploit it for political purposes.

THE ORGANIZATION OF LATE IMPERIAL CHRISTIANITY

Many Roman provincials were Christian higher clergy. Between the legalization of Christianity by Constantine about 313 and the adoption of Christianity as the legal religion of Rome by the emperor Theodosius I in 380, Christian communities received immense donations of land, labour, and other gifts from emperors and wealthy converts. The Christian clergy, originally a body of community elders and managerial functionaries, gradually acquired sacramental authority and became aligned with the grades of the imperial civil service. Each *civitas* (community or city), an urban unit and its surrounding district, had its bishop (from the Latin *episcopus*, "overseer"). Because there had been more Roman *civitates* in the Italian and provincial European areas, there were more and usually smaller dioceses in these regions than in the distant north and east.

During the 5th and 6th centuries, bishops gradually assumed greater responsibility for supplying the cities and administering their affairs, replacing the local governments that for centuries had underpinned and constituted the local administration of the empire. Two bishops, Ambrose of Milan (339–397) and Gregory I of Rome (pope 590–604), wrote influential guidebooks on episcopal and other clerical duties and responsibilities toward congregations. These works set standards for all later bishops and are still observed in many churches.

Besides the bishops and their subordinates the priests, who tended to the spiritual and material needs of Christians living in the world—the "secular clergy"—there also existed communities of monks and religious women who had fled the world. These communities were independent, although nominally under the control of the local bishop, and they followed diverse rules of life—hence their designation as "regular clergy" (from *regula*, "rule"). The most influential monastic rule in Latin Christianity after the 8th century was that of Benedict of Nursia (*c.* 480–*c.* 547). Benedict's rule provided for a monastic day of work, prayer, and contemplation, offering psychological balance in the monk's life. It also elevated the dignity of manual labour in the service of God, long scorned by the elites of antiquity. Benedict's monastery at Monte

Cassino, south of Rome, became one of the greatest centres of Benedictine monasticism.

The origins of monasticism lay in Egyptian and Syrian monks' ascetic practices, which were transplanted to western Europe through texts such as the 4th-century Latin translation of the *Life of Saint Antony* (by Patriarch Athanasius of Alexandria) and through widely traveled observers such as the theologian and monk John Cassian (360–435). These Mediterranean-wide influences were among the last examples of the communications network of the older, ecumenical Mediterranean world. Monasticism developed and sustained a powerful ascetic dimension in both Greek and Latin Christianity that increased in importance as monasticism itself came to define the ideal of clerical life in the West.

In the case of Martin (316–397), a former Roman soldier turned wandering holy man, monastic asceticism was combined with the office episcopal, as Martin eventually became bishop of Tours in Gaul. He emphasized the conversion of rural pagans, as well as ministering to the urban and rural elites. In the Iberian Peninsula the work of the monk and bishop Martin of Braga (*c.* 515–580) was also devoted to the religious instruction of rustics. His work provided an influential model for the later conversion of northern and eastern Europe.

While Greek Christians called their church and religion Orthodox, Latin Christians adopted the term Catholic (from *catholicus*, "universal"). The term *catholic Christianity* was originally used to authenticate a normative, orthodox Christian cult (system of religious belief and ritual) on the grounds of its universality and to characterize different beliefs and practices as heterodox on the grounds that they were merely local and did not reflect duration, unanimity, or universality. These three characteristics of Latin orthodoxy were defined by the

5th-century monastic writer Vincent of Lérins (died *c.* 450) and adopted generally throughout the Latin church.

Devotional movements that differed from the norms of orthodoxy were defined as heterodoxy, or heresy. The earliest of these were several forms of Judaizing Christianity and Gnosticism, a dualist belief in asceticism and spiritual enlightenment. Once Christianity was established throughout the empire, other local movements were also condemned. Donatism, the belief among many North African Christians that Christian leaders who had bowed to pagan imperial persecution before 313 had lost their priestly status and needed to be reordained, was the first major heterodox practice to be considered—and condemned—at an imperial church council (411). Other movements were Arianism, which challenged the divinity of Jesus, and Pelagianism, which denied original sin and emphasized purely human abilities to achieve salvation. Other beliefs, usually those that contradicted increasingly normative doctrines of Trinitarianism (the belief that the Godhead includes three coequal, coeternal, and consubstantial persons) or Christology (the interpretation of the nature of Christ), were also condemned as heresy.

Normative Christianity, which was expressed in imperial legislation, church councils, and the works of influential Christian writers, gradually became the faith of Europe's new regional rulers. Within that broad, universal ideology, however, many of the new kings and peoples based their claims to legitimacy and a common identity on their own versions of Latin Christianity, as expressed in local law, ritual, saints' cults, sacred spaces and shrines, and saints' relics. The cults of saints and their relics served to territorialize devotion, and control over them was a distinctive sign of legitimate power. Although the older empire and the new, nonimperial lands in Europe into

Monasticism

Monasticism is an institutionalized religious practice or movement whose members attempt to live by a rule that requires works that go beyond those of either the laity or the ordinary spiritual leaders of their religions. Commonly celibate and universally ascetic, the monastic individual separates himself or herself from society either by living as a hermit or anchorite (religious recluse) or by joining a community (*coenobium*) of others who profess similar intentions. First applied to Christian groups, both Latin and Greek, the term monasticism is now used to denote similar, though not identical, practices in religions such as Buddhism, Hinduism, Jainism, and Daoism.

The word monasticism is derived from the Greek *monachos* ("living alone"), but this etymology highlights only one of the elements of monasticism and is somewhat misleading, because a large proportion of the world's monastics live in cenobitic (common life) communities. The term monasticism implies celibacy, or living alone in the sense of lacking a spouse, which became a socially and historically crucial feature of the monastic life.

A Benedictine monk restoring late-medieval books at the monastery of Monte Oliveto Maggiore, Tuscany, Italy. © Pedro Coll/A.G.E. FotoStock

which a new culture expanded came to call themselves
Christianitas ("Christendom"), they were in practice
divided into many self-contained entities that have been
called "micro-Christendoms," each based on the devotional identity of king, clerics, and people.

KINGS AND PEOPLES

The kings of new peoples ruled as much in Roman style
as they could, issuing laws written in Latin for their own
peoples and their Roman subjects and striking coins
that imitated imperial coinage. They also sponsored the
composition of "ethnic" and genealogical histories that
attributed to themselves and their peoples, however
recently assembled, an identity and antiquity rivaling that
of Rome. Although the Romans, who called their own
society a *populus* ("civil people"), used the term *rex* ("king")
only for rulers of peoples at lower levels of sociocultural
development, the political order of kings and peoples
became a commonplace in Europe in late antiquity and
would remain so until the 19th century. Some of these
kingdoms, especially that of the Visigoths in southern
Gaul and later in Iberia, also modeled themselves on the
ancient Hebrew kingdoms as described in Scripture. They
borrowed and adapted some ancient Jewish rituals, such
as liturgically anointing the ruler with oil and reminding
him in sermons, prayers, and meetings of church councils that he was God's servant, with spiritual and political
responsibilities that legitimized his power.

As the cultures associated with the new kings and peoples spread throughout western Europe from the 5th to
the 8th centuries, they influenced political and religious
change in areas that the empire had never ruled—initially
Ireland, then northern Britain, the lower Rhineland, and
trans-Rhenish Europe (the lands east of the Rhine River).

The bishop and the monk were two of the most remarkable and longest enduring religious and social inventions of late antiquity; the barbarian kingdoms were a third. Although many of the latter did not survive, their experiments in Christian kingship, as represented in texts, ritual, pictures, and objects, began a long tradition in European political life and thought.

THE GREAT COMMISSION

The process of expansion was also driven by a missionary mandate. Reflecting a new, literal, and personal understanding of Jesus' command in the Gospels to baptize and to proclaim the word of God (Matthew 28:19; Mark 16:15), the work of conversion to Christianity was extended to all peoples, not just to those of the empire. Conversion was carried out at first by individual Christians acting on their own, not as agents of an organized church. Greek Christians from Constantinople also undertook missionary work, sometimes individually but also as an increasingly prominent aspect of Byzantine imperial diplomacy in the Balkans and north of the Danube valley and the Black Sea. In the eastern parts of the Byzantine Empire, communities of Nestorian Christians, who stressed the independence of the human and divine persons of Christ, moved beyond the imperial frontiers, first into Persia and then farther east. By the 10th century a long string of such settlements ran along the Silk Road from the Mediterranean to China.

Individual conversion stories were modeled on that of St. Paul the Apostle (Acts of the Apostles 9–10), which itself was echoed in the *Confessions* of St. Augustine. Individual conversion experiences touched people in all walks of life: Martin of Tours, the soldier turned ascetic and bishop; the Gallo-Roman aristocrats Sulpicius Severus—who wrote about the influential life of Martin—and Caesarius of Arles;

and the free Romano-Briton St. Patrick, who had been a slave in pagan Ireland and returned to convert his former captors.

But the most widely accepted model of conversion of both religious belief and practice was collective—that of a ruler and his followers together as a new Christian people. In this way, the king and church integrated rulership with clerical teaching and the development of the liturgy and with the definition of sacred space, control of sanctity, and the rituals surrounding key moments in human life, from baptism to death and burial. The most notable of the collective conversions were that of the Visigoths from Arian to Catholic Christianity in 589, that of the Frankish leader Clovis by his Catholic Burgundian wife Clotilda and the Gallo-Roman bishop Remigius of Reims about the turn of the 6th century, and that of Aethelberht of Kent by St. Augustine of Canterbury.

As Romans and non-Romans locally assimilated into new peoples during the 6th and 7th centuries, non-Romans, as had Romans before them, became Christian monks, higher clergy, and sometimes saints. In the late 5th century the conversion of Ireland, the first Christianized territory that had never been part of the Roman Empire, brought the particularly Irish ascetic practice of self-exile to bear on missionary work. In the 6th century the Irish monk Columba (c. 521–597) exiled himself to the island of Iona, from which he began to convert the peoples of southwestern Scotland. Other Irish monk-exiles moved through the Rhine Valley, Austria, Bavaria, Switzerland, and northern Italy. Columban (c. 543–615), the most influential of these missionaries, greatly reformed the devotional life of the Frankish nobility and founded monasteries at Sankt Gallen, Luxeuil, and Bobbio. Irish and Scottish devotional practices also influenced England, where Celtic forms of Christianity clashed with Continental, especially Roman, forms—a conflict resolved at the Synod of

Whitby in 663/664, when Roman norms were adopted first for the kingdom of Northumbria and later for other English kingdoms. Irish influence remained strong in the English church, however, especially in matters of learning, church reform, missionary exile, and clerical organization.

From the late 7th century, English pilgrims visited Rome, creating a strong devotional link between Rome and Britain, which was reasserted wherever English missionary activity took place. Benedict Biscop, an English noble, traveled to Rome several times, returning with Roman books and pictures. He founded the twin monasteries of Wearmouth and Jarrow (the saintly scholar Bede was a monk of Wearmouth-Jarrow) and escorted the learned Theodore of Tarsus back to England when Theodore was appointed archbishop of Canterbury. Theodore's pastoral and educational activities greatly enhanced English clerical culture, producing both a network of schools and a missionary consciousness that sent English monks, like their Irish predecessors, to the Continent. The most influential of these figures was Boniface (c. 675–754), the first archbishop of Mainz, who spent much of his adult life in missionary and reform work in and around the edges of the kingdom of the Franks. The letters of Boniface demonstrate his respect for Rome and provide important information about his missionary activities. His great monastery of Fulda played an important role in both reform and conversion.

THE BISHOPS OF ROME

Throughout their history, the bishops of Rome enjoyed great respect and veneration because of the antiquity of their see, its historical orthodoxy, the relics of its martyrs (including Saints Peter and Paul the Apostles), and the imperial and Christian history of the city of Rome. The

Synod of Whitby

The Christian church of the Anglo-Saxon kingdom of Northumbria convened the Synod of Whitby in 663/664 to decide whether to follow Celtic or Roman usages. The meeting marked a vital turning point in the development of the church in England.

Though Northumbria had been mainly converted by Celtic missionaries, there was by 662 a Roman party, which included Queen Eanfled, Bishop Wilfrid, and other influential people. The Celtic party was led by the bishops Colman and Cedd and Abbess Hilda. Two accounts of the synod survive, in Bede's *Ecclesiastical History of the English People* and in the life of Wilfrid by the monk Eddi. King Oswiu decided in favour of Rome because he believed that Rome followed the teaching of St. Peter, the holder of the keys of heaven. The decision led to the acceptance of Roman usage elsewhere in England and brought the English Church into close contact with the Continent.

material conditions of the 6th and 7th centuries, however, greatly limited any papal exercise of universal authority or influence, and the popes developed relatively little theory about papal authority of any kind over all Christians. Like other bishops, however, the bishops of Rome benefited from the idea of *traditio* (Latin: "tradition"), which stated that the authority of the Apostles had been passed down to the Christian higher clergy. They also gradually assumed more and more responsibility for the administration of the city itself. Because Rome was Rome and because the properties of the Roman church extended throughout Italy, the papal administration of the city and the invocation of its Christian, rather than imperial, past slowly turned it into the Rome of St. Peter, who accordingly assumed an increasingly important role in medieval spirituality. This Christianized Rome was a place that the diversified societies of western Europe could revere and visit because of its devotional centrality in the Latin Christian world.

Pope Gregory the Great receiving information from the Holy Spirit, represented as a dove, carved ivory book cover, c. 980; in the Kunsthistorisches Museum, Vienna. Kunsthistorisches Museum, Vienna

Between the 5th and the 11th century, many argued that, just as there had been a hierarchy of cities in the old empire, there was a hierarchy of bishops, and the bishop of Rome stood at its head. Although the idea of papal supremacy in Latin Christendom found a number of papal and nonpapal exponents during this period, it did not become dominant until the late 11th century. Even before then, however, the affection and respect for Rome built up in England and in the kingdom of the Franks did much to increase the attractiveness of the papacy.

THE MEDITERRANEAN WORLD DIVIDED

During the 7th and 8th centuries, new invasions of the eastern part of the empire and the emergence of Islam, first in the Arabian Peninsula and then to the west in Egypt and Numidia and to the east in Persia, divided the old Mediterranean ecumenical world into three distinct culture zones: East Rome, or Byzantium; Islam; and Latin Europe. Byzantium and western Europe remained long on the defensive against Islamic pressures, which extended to the conquest of the Iberian Peninsula in 711, Sicily in 902, and Anatolia in the 11th century. Each of these three cultures developed its own character based on different uses of and attitudes toward the Roman-Mediterranean ecumenical past. They maintained diplomatic and commercial contact with each other, though sometimes on a much-reduced scale, and continued to influence each other culturally even as they became more distinct. In spite of their increasing distinctiveness, they were never entirely separated, since both trade and the transmission of ideas passed through their porous edges. In addition, large numbers of Jews and Christians continued to live as privileged religious aliens in most of the Muslim world.

THE FRANKISH ASCENDANCY

In the late 5th and early 6th centuries, Clovis I (*c.* 466–511), the warrior-leader of one of the groups of peoples collectively known as the Franks, established a strong independent monarchy in what are now the northern part of France and the southwestern part of Belgium. He expanded into southern Gaul, driving the Visigoths across the Pyrenees, and established a strong Frankish presence east of the Rhine. His power was recognized by the eastern emperor Anastasius, who made him a Roman consul (a high-ranking magistrate). In the generations following the death of Clovis, the Frankish kingdom was often divided into the two kingdoms of Neustria and Austrasia, though it was occasionally reunited under Clovis's successors, the Merovingian dynasty. It was later reunited under the lordship and (after 751) monarchy of the eastern Frankish Arnulfing-Pippinid family (later known as the Carolingian dynasty), which included Pippin II and his successors Charles Martel, Pippin III, and Charlemagne (reigned 768–814). This dynasty brought much of western Europe under Frankish control and established diplomatic relations with Britain, Iberia, Rome, Constantinople, Christians in the Holy Land, and even Hārūn al-Rashīd, the great caliph in Baghdad.

CHARLEMAGNE AND THE CAROLINGIAN DYNASTY

Charlemagne and his successors patronized a vast project that they and their clerical advisers called *correctio*—restoring the fragmented western European world to an earlier idealized condition. During the Carolingian Renaissance, as it is called by modern scholars, Frankish rulers supported monastic studies and manuscript production, attempted to standardize monastic practice

Merovingian Dynasty

The Merovingians were a Frankish dynasty that traditionally has been reckoned as the "first race" of the kings of France. The name Merovingian derives from that of Merovech, of whom nothing is known except that he was the father of Childeric I, who ruled a tribe of Salian Franks from his capital at Tournai. Childeric was succeeded by his son Clovis I in 481 or 482. Clovis I extended his rule over all the Salian Franks, conquered or annexed the territories of the Ripuarian Franks and the Alemanni, and united nearly all of Gaul except for Burgundy and what is now Provence. Of equal importance, he was converted to Christianity in either 496 or 506. At Clovis I's death in 511, his realm was divided among his four sons, Theuderic I, Chlodomir, Childebert I, and Chlotar I. Despite the frequently bloody competition between the brothers, they managed among them to extend Frankish rule over Thuringia in approximately 531 and Burgundy in 534 and to gain sway over, if not possession of, Septimania on the Mediterranean coast, Bavaria, and the lands of the Saxons to the north. By 558 Chlotar I was the last surviving son of Clovis I, and until his death in 561 the Frankish realm was once again united.

In 561 the realm was again divided between brothers—Charibert I, Guntram, Sigebert, and Chilperic I—and again family strife and intrigue ensued, particularly between Chilperic and his wife, Fredegund, in the northwest of Gaul and Sigebert and his wife, Brunhild, in the northeast. Dynastic struggles and increasing pressures exerted on the realm by neighbouring peoples—Bretons and Gascons in the west, Lombards in the southeast, Avars in the east—prompted a reorganization of the Frankish kingdoms. Several eastern regions were merged into the kingdom of Austrasia, with its capital at Metz; in the west Neustria emerged, with its capital first at Soissons and later at Paris; to the south was the enlarged kingdom of Burgundy, with its capital at Chalon-sur-Saône. Overall Frankish unity was again achieved in 613, when Chlotar II, son of Chilperic I and king of Neustria, inherited the other two kingdoms as well. On the death of Chlotar's son Dagobert I in 639, the realm was divided yet again, but by that time the kings of the two regions, Neustria and Burgundy on the one hand and Austrasia on the other, had been forced to yield much of their power to household officials known as mayors of the palace. The later Merovingian kings were little more than puppets and were enthroned and deposed at will by powerful mayors of the palace. The last Merovingian, Childeric III, was deposed in 750 by Pippin III the Short, one of a line of Austrasian mayors of the palace who finally usurped the throne itself to establish the Carolingian dynasty.

and rules of life, insisted on high moral and educational standards for clergy, adopted and disseminated standard versions of canon law and the liturgy, and maintained a regular network of communications throughout their dominions.

Charlemagne drew heavily on most of the kingdoms of Christian Europe, even those he conquered, for many of his advisers. Ireland sent Dicuil the geographer. The kingdoms of Anglo-Saxon England, drawn close to Rome and the Franks during the 8th century, produced the widely circulated works of Bede and the ecclesiastical reformer Boniface. Also from England was the scholar Alcuin, a product of the great school at York, who served as Charlemagne's chief adviser on ecclesiastical and other matters until becoming abbot of the monastery of St. Martin of Tours. Charlemagne's relations with the kingdoms in England remained cordial, and his political and intellectual reforms in turn shaped the development of a unified English monarchy and culture under Alfred (reigned 871–899) and his successors in the 9th and 10th centuries.

Although the Visigothic kingdom fell to Arab and Berber armies in 711, the small Christian principalities in the north of the Iberian Peninsula held out. They too produced remarkable scholars, some of whom were eventually judged to hold heretical beliefs. The Christological theology of adoptionism, which held that Christ in his

St. Mark, illuminated manuscript page from the Gospel book of the court school of Charlemagne, c. 810; in the Stadtbibliothek, Trier, Ger. Stadtbibliothek, Trier, Ger.

humanity is the adopted son of God, greatly troubled the Carolingian court and generated a substantial literature on both sides before the belief was declared heterodox. But Iberia also produced scholars for Charlemagne's service, particularly Theodulf of Orleans, one of the emperor's most influential advisers.

The kingdom of the Lombards, established in northern and central Italy in the later 6th century, was originally Arian but converted to Catholic Christianity in the 7th century. Nevertheless, Lombard opposition to Byzantine forces in northern Italy and Lombard pressure on the bishops of Rome led a number of 8th-century popes to call on the assistance of the Carolingians. Pippin invaded Italy twice in the 750s, and in 774 Charlemagne conquered the Lombard kingdom and assumed its crown. Among the Lombards who migrated for a time to Charlemagne's court were the grammarian Peter of Pisa and the historian Paul the Deacon.

From 778 to 803 Charlemagne not only stabilized his rule in Frankland and Italy but also conquered and converted the Saxons and established frontier commands, or marches, at the most vulnerable edges of his territories. He built a residence for himself and his court at Aachen, which was called "a second Rome." He remained on excellent terms with the bishops of Rome, Adrian I (reigned 772–795) and Leo III (reigned 795–816). Scholars began to call Charlemagne "the father of Europe" and "the lighthouse of Europe." Although the lands under his rule were often referred to as "the kingdom of Europe," contemporaries recognized them as forming an empire, much of which extended well beyond the imperial frontiers of Rome. Because of its use in reference to the empire, the old geographical term Europe came to be invested with a political and cultural meaning that it did not have in Greco-Roman antiquity.

In 800 Charlemagne extracted Leo III from severe political difficulties in Rome (Leo had been violently attacked by relatives of the former pope and accused of various crimes). On Christmas Day of that year Leo crowned Charlemagne emperor of the Romans, a title that Charlemagne's successors also adopted. Although the title gave Charlemagne no resources that he did not already possess, it did not please all his subjects, and it greatly displeased the Byzantines. But it survived the Frankish monarchy and remained the most respected title of a lay ruler in Europe until the Holy Roman Empire, as it was known from the mid-12th century, was abolished by Napoleon Bonaparte in 1806, a little more than 1,000 years after Charlemagne was crowned. Historians still debate whether the coronation of 800 indicated a backward-looking last manifestation of the older world of late antiquity or a new organization of the elements of what later became Europe.

Charlemagne's kingdoms, but not the imperial title, were divided after the death of his son Louis I (the Pious) in 840 into the regions of West Francia, the Middle Kingdom, and East Francia. The last of these regions gradually assumed control over the Middle Kingdom north of the Alps. In addition, an independent kingdom of Italy survived into the late 10th century. The imperial title went to one of the rulers of these kingdoms, usually the one who could best protect Rome, until it briefly ceased to be used in the early 10th century.

CAROLINGIAN DECLINE AND ITS CONSEQUENCES

After the Carolingian dynasty died out in the male line in East Francia in 911, Conrad I, the first of a series of territorial dukes, was elected king. He was followed by a series of vigorous and ambitious rulers from the Saxon (919–1024) and Salian (1024–1125) dynasties. Otto I (reigned 936–967), the most successful of the Saxon rulers, claimed the crown of the old Lombard kingdom in Italy in 951, defeated an invading Hungarian army at the Battle of Lechfeld in 955, and was crowned emperor in Rome in 962. In contrast to the kings of East Francia, the rulers of West Francia, whose last Carolingian ruler was succeeded in 987 by the long-lasting dynasty of Hugh Capet (the Capetian dynasty), had difficulty ruling even their domains in the middle Seine valley, and they were overshadowed by the power of the territorial lords who had established themselves in principalities in the rest of the kingdom.

The end of Carolingian expansion in the early 9th century and the inability of several kings to field sufficiently large armies and reward their followers were two consequences of the division of Charlemagne's empire. In addition, the empire now shared borders with hostile peoples in the Slavic east and in the Low Countries, Scandinavia, and Iberia. The end of expansion meant that the basis of the economy shifted from mixed forest-agricultural labour and income drawn from plunder and tribute to more-intensive cultivation of lands within the kingdoms. Accordingly, kings were forced to draw on local resources to reward their followers. The consequences of these military and economic changes included a general weakening of royal authority, the transformation of the Carolingian aristocracy into active lords of the land, and a loss of social status for the labourers who worked the land.

In the 9th and early 10th centuries a series of invasions from Scandinavia, the lower Danube valley, and North Africa greatly weakened the Carolingian world. The divisions within the Frankish empire impaired its ability to resist the Viking and Hungarian invasions but did not destroy it. Kings and warlords ultimately either turned back the invaders, as Otto I did in 955, or absorbed them into their territories, as the kings of West Francia did with the Vikings in Normandy. In England the invasions destroyed all of the older kingdoms except Wessex, whose rulers, starting with Alfred, expanded their power until they created a single kingdom of England.

Although two kinds of invaders—the Scandinavians and the Hungarians—became acculturated and Christianized during the next several centuries, creating the Christian kingdoms of Norway, Denmark, Sweden, and Hungary, the Islamic world remained apart, extending from Iberia and Morocco eastward to the western edges of China and Southeast Asia. In the case of western Europe, the attacks of the 9th and 10th centuries were the last outside invasions until the Allied landings during World War II; indeed, for a period of nearly 1,000 years western Europe was the only part of the world that was not invaded. Western Europe developed internally without outside interference, expanded geographically, increased demographically, improved materially, and engaged in cultural, commercial, and technological exchanges with parallel civilizations.

GROWTH AND INNOVATION

Although historians disagree about the extent of the social and material damage caused by the 9th- and 10th-century invasions, they agree that demographic growth began during the 10th century and perhaps earlier. They have also identified signs of the reorganization of lordship and agricultural labour, a process in which members of an order of experienced and determined warriors concentrated control of land in their own hands and coerced a largely free peasantry into subjection. Thus did the idea of the three orders of society—those who fight, those who pray, and those who labour—come into use to describe the results of the ascendancy of the landholding aristocracy and its clerical partners. In cooperation with bishops and ecclesiastical establishments, particularly great monastic foundations such as Cluny (established 910), the nobility of the late 11th and 12th centuries reorganized the agrarian landscape and rural society of western Europe and made it the base of urbanization, which was also well under way in the 11th century.

DEMOGRAPHIC AND AGRICULTURAL GROWTH

It has been estimated that between 1000 and 1340 the population of Europe increased from about 38.5 million people to about 73.5 million, with the greatest proportional increase occurring in northern Europe, which trebled its population. The rate of growth was not so rapid as to create a crisis of overpopulation; it was linked to increased agricultural production, which yielded a sufficient amount of food per capita, permitted the expansion of cultivated land, and enabled some of the population to become non-agricultural workers, thereby creating a new division of labour and greater economic and cultural diversity.

The late Roman countryside and its patterns of life—a social pattern of landlords, free peasants, half-free workers, and slaves and an economic pattern of cultivated fields and orchards and the use of thick forests and their products—survived well into the Carolingian period. In the late 9th century, however, political circumstances led landholders to intensify the cultivation of their lands. They did this by reducing the status of formerly free peasants to dependent servitude and by slowly elevating the status of slaves to the same dependency, creating a rural society of serfs. The old Latin word for slave, *servus*, now came to designate a category of rural workers who were not chattel property but who were firmly bound to their lord's land. The new word for slave, *sclavus*, was derived from the source of many slaves, the Slavic lands of the east. During the 11th and 12th centuries the chief social distinction in western European society was that between the free and the unfree. For two centuries the status of serfdom was imposed on people whose ancestors had been free and who themselves would become free only when the rise of a money economy in the late 12th century made free, rent-paying peasants more economically attractive to lords than bound serfs. The aristocracy was able to accomplish this because of weakening royal power and generosity and because of its assumption of the *bannum* ("ban"), the old public and largely royal power to command and punish (now called "banal jurisdiction"). It announced its new claims by calling them "customs" and adjudicated them in local courts.

The aristocracy supervised the clearing of forest for the expansion of cereal cultivation but restricted the remaining forest to itself for hunting. It also forced its dependents to use its mills and local markets, to provide various labour services, and to settle more densely in the villages, which were slowly coordinated with an expanded system of parishes (local churches with lay patrons, to which peasants had to pay the tithe, or one-tenth of their produce). Serfdom was gradually eliminated in western Europe during the 13th and 14th centuries as a result of economic changes that made agricultural labour less financially advantageous to lords. During the same period, however, serfdom increased in eastern Europe, where it lasted until the 19th century.

The new stratification of society into the categories of free and unfree was accompanied by the transformation of the late Carolingian aristocratic family from a widespread association of both paternal and maternal relatives to a narrower lineage, in which paternal ancestry and paternal control of the disposition of inheritance dominated. Family memory restricted itself to a founding paternal ancestor, ignoring the line of maternal ancestors, and the new lineages identified themselves with a principal piece of property, from which they often took a family name. They also patronized religious establishments, which memorialized the families in prayers, enhanced their local prestige, and often provided them burial in their precincts.

The new lords of the land identified themselves primarily as warriors. Because new technologies of warfare, including heavy cavalry, were expensive, fighting men required substantial material resources as well as considerable leisure to train. The economic and political transformation of the countryside filled these two needs. The old armies of free men of different levels of wealth were replaced by new

English axman in combat with Norman mounted knight during the Battle of Hastings, detail from the 11th-century Bayeux Tapestry; in the Musée de la Tapisserie de la Reine-Mathilde, in the former Bishop's Palace, Bayeux, France. Giraudon/Art Resource, New York

armies of specialist knights. The term *knight* (Latin *miles*) came into more frequent use to designate anyone who could satisfy the new military requirements, which included the wealthiest and most powerful lords as well as fighting men from far lower levels of society. The new order gradually developed its own ethos, reflected in the ideal of chivalry, the knight's code of conduct. The distinction between free and unfree was reinforced by the distinction between those who fought, even at the lowest level, and those who could not. Those who functioned at the lowest level of military service worked hard to distinguish themselves from those who laboured in the fields.

TECHNOLOGICAL INNOVATIONS

The increases in population and agricultural productivity were accompanied by a technological revolution that introduced new sources of power and a cultural "machine-mindedness," both of which were incorporated into a wide spectrum of economic enterprises. The chief new sources of power were the horse, the water mill, and the windmill. Europeans began to breed both the specialized warhorse, adding stirrups to provide the mounted warrior a better seat and greater striking force, and the draft horse, now shod with iron horseshoes that protected the hooves from the damp clay soils of northern Europe. The draft horse was faster and more efficient than the ox, the traditional beast of burden. The invention of the new horse collar in the 10th century, a device that pulled from the horse's shoulders rather than from its neck and windpipe, immeasurably increased the animal's pulling power.

The extensive network of rivers in western Europe spurred the development of the water mill, not only for grinding grain into flour but also by the 12th century for converting simple rotary motion into reciprocal motion.

Where water was not readily available, Europeans constructed windmills, which had been imported from the Middle East, thereby spreading the mill to even more remote locations.

In heavily forested and mountainous parts of western Europe, foresters, charcoal burners, and miners formed separate communities, providing timber, fuel, and metallic ores in abundance. The demands of domestic and public building and shipbuilding threatened to deforest much of Europe as early as the 13th century. Increasingly refined metallurgical technology produced not only well-tempered swords, daggers, and armour for warriors but also elaborate domestic ware. Glazed pottery and glass also appeared even in humble homes, which were increasingly built of stone rather than wood and thatch.

The most striking and familiar examples of the technological revolution are the great Gothic cathedrals and other churches, which were constructed from the 12th century onward. Universally admired for their soaring height and stained-glass windows, they required mathematically precise designs; considerable understanding of the properties of subsoils, stone, and timber; near-professional architectural skills; complex financial planning; and a skilled labour force. They are generally regarded as the most-accomplished engineering feats of the Middle Ages.

URBAN GROWTH

The experience of building great churches was replicated in the development of the material fabric of the new and expanded cities. The cities of the Carolingian world were few and small. Their functions were limited to serving the needs of the kings, bishops, or monasteries that inhabited them. Some, especially those that were close to the Mediterranean, were reconfigured Roman cities. In

the north a Roman nucleus sometimes became the core
of a new city, but just as often cities emerged because of
the needs of their lords. The northern cities were established as local market centres and then developed into
centres of diversified artisanal production with growing
merchant populations. In the 10th and 11th centuries new
cities were founded and existing cities increased in area
and population. They were usually enclosed within a wall
once their inhabitants thought that the city had reached
the limits of its expansion; as populations grew and sub-
urbs began to surround the walls, many cities built new
and larger walls to enclose the new space. The succession
of concentric rings of town walls offers a history of urban
growth in many cities. Inhabitants also took pride in their
city's appearance, as evidenced by the elaborate decora-
tions on city gates, fountains, town halls (in northern Italy
from the 10th century), and other public spaces. Cities
were cultural as well as economic and political centres,
and their decoration was as important to their inhabitants
as their water systems, defenses, and marketplaces.

The cities attracted people from the countryside,
where the increasing productivity of the farms was freeing
many peasants from working on the land. Various mercantile and craft guilds were formed beginning in the 10th
century to protect their members' common interests. The
merchants' guilds and other associations also contributed
to the emergence of the sworn commune, or the self-reg-
ulating city government, originally chartered by a bishop,
count, or king. The city distinguished itself from the countryside, even as it extended its influence there. During the
12th century this distinction was recognized culturally,
when the Latin word *urbanitas* ("urbanity") came to be
applied to the idea of acceptable manners and informed
Christian belief, while *rusticitas* ("rusticity") came to mean
inelegance and backwardness. Despite this awareness,

cities had to protect their food supplies and their trade and communication routes, and thus in both southern and northern Europe the city and its *contado* (region surrounding the city) became closely linked.

In some areas of northern Europe, particular kinds of manufacturing became prominent, especially dyeing, weaving, and finishing woolen cloth. Wool production was the economic enterprise in which the cities of the southern Low Countries took pride of place, and other cities developed elaborate manufacturing of metalwork and armaments. Still others became market centres of essential products that could not be produced locally, such as wine. This specialized production led to the proliferation of long-range trade and the creation of communications networks along the rivers of western Europe, where many cities were located. Although some lords, including the kings of England, were reluctant to recognize the towns' autonomy, most eventually agreed that the rapidly increasing value of the towns as centres of manufacturing and trade was worth the risk of their practical independence.

Originally a product of the agrarian dynamic that shaped society after the year 1000, the growing towns of western Europe became increasingly important, and their citizens acquired great wealth, usually in cooperation rather than conflict with their rulers. The towns helped transform the agrarian world out of which they were originally created into a precapitalist manufacturing and market economy that influenced both urban and rural development.

REFORM AND RENEWAL

A number of the movements for ecclesiastical reform that emerged in the 11th century attempted to sharpen the distinction between clerical and lay status. Most of these movements drew upon the older Christian ideas of

spiritual renewal and reform, which were thought necessary because of the degenerative effects of the passage of
time on fallen human nature. They also drew upon standards of monastic conduct, especially those regarding
celibacy and devotional rigour, that had been articulated
during the Carolingian period and were now extended to
all clergy, regular (monks) and secular (priests). Virginity,
long seen by Christian thinkers as an equivalent to mar-
tyrdom, was now required of all clergy. It has been argued
that the requirement of celibacy was established to protect ecclesiastical property, which had greatly increased,
from being alienated by the clergy or from becoming the
basis of dynastic power. The doctrine of clerical celibacy
and freedom from sexual pollution, the idea that the clergy
should not be dependent on the laity, and the insistence
on the *libertas* ("liberty") of the church—the freedom to
accomplish its divinely ordained mission without interference from any secular authority—became the basis of the
reform movements that took shape during this period.
Most of them originated in reforming monasteries in
transalpine Europe, which cooperative lay patrons and
supporters protected from predatory violence.

By the middle of the 11th century, the reform movements reached Rome itself, when the emperor Henry III
intervened in a schism that involved three claimants to the
papal throne. At the Synod of Sutri in 1046 he appointed a
transalpine candidate of his own—Suidger, archbishop of
Bamberg, who became Pope Clement II (1046–47)—and
removed the papal office from the influence of the local
Roman nobility, which had largely controlled it since the
10th century. A series of popes, including Leo IX (1049–
54) and Urban II (1088–99), promoted what is known as
Gregorian Reform, named for its most zealous proponent,
Pope Gregory VII (1073–85). They urged reform throughout Europe by means of their official correspondence and

their sponsorship of regional church councils. They also restructured the hierarchy, placing the papal office at the head of reform efforts and articulating a systematic claim to papal authority over clergy and, in very many matters, over laity as well.

The emotional intensity of ecclesiastical reform led to outbursts of religious enthusiasm from both supporters and opponents. Many laypeople also enthusiastically supported reform; indeed, their support was a key factor in its ultimate success. The increase in lay piety on the side of reform was indicated by the events of 1095, when Urban II called on lay warriors to cease preying on the weak and on each other and to undertake the liberation of the Holy Land from its Muslim conquerors and occupiers. The enormous military expedition that captured Jerusalem in 1099 and established for a century the Latin kingdom of Jerusalem, an expedition only much later called the First Crusade, is as dramatic a sign as possible of the vitality and devotion of clerical and lay reformers.

The First Crusade had other, unintended effects. The success of Genoa, Pisa, and other Italian maritime cities in supplying the Christian outposts in the Holy Land increased their already considerable wealth and political power, which were soon comparable to that of Venice. Proposals for later Crusades often led to searching analyses, not only of specific military, financial, and logistical requirements but also of the social reforms that such ventures would require in the kingdoms of Europe. Finally, by bringing Latin Christians other than pilgrims deeper into western Eurasia than they had ever been before, the Crusade movement led Europeans in the 12th century to a greater interest in distant parts of the world.

The reform movement had a pronounced effect on church and society. It produced an independent clerical order, hierarchically organized under the popes. The clergy claimed both a teaching authority (magisterium) and a disciplinary authority, based on theology and canon law, that defined orthodoxy and heterodoxy and regulated much of lay and all of clerical life. The clergy also expressed its authority through a series of energetic church councils, from the first Lateran Council in 1123 to the fourth Lateran Council in 1215, and greatly enhanced both the ritual and legal authority of the popes.

The reform movement also erupted in a violent conflict, known as the Investiture Controversy, between Gregory VII and the emperor Henry IV (reigned 1056–1105/06). In this struggle the pope claimed extraordinary authority to correct the emperor; he twice declared the emperor deposed before Henry forced him to flee Rome to Salerno, where he died in exile. Despite Gregory's apparent defeat, the conflicts undermined imperial claims to authority and shattered the Carolingian-Ottonian image of the emperor as the lay equal of the bishop of Rome, responsible for acting in worldly matters to protect the church. The emperor, like any other layman, was now subordinate to the moral discipline of churchmen.

Some later emperors, notably the members of the Hohenstaufen dynasty—including Frederick I Barbarossa (1152–90), his son Henry VI (1190–97), and his grandson Frederick II (1220–50)—reasserted modified claims for imperial authority and intervened in Italy with some success. But Barbarossa's political ambitions were thwarted by the northern Italian cities of the Lombard League and the forces of Pope Alexander III at the Battle of Legnano in 1176. Both Henry VI and Frederick II, who had united the imperial and Lombard crowns and added to them that of the rich and powerful Norman kingdom of Sicily, were checked by similar resistance. Frederick himself was deposed by Pope Innocent IV in 1245. Succession disputes following Frederick's death and that of his immediate successors led to the Great Interregnum of 1250–73, when no candidate received enough electoral votes to become emperor. The interregnum ended only with the election of the Habsburg ruler Rudolf I (1273–91), which resulted in the increasing provincialization of the imperial office in favour of Habsburg dynastic and territorial interests. In 1356 the Luxembourg emperor Charles IV (1316–78) issued the Golden Bull, which established the number of imperial electors at seven (three ecclesiastical and four lay princes) and articulated their powers.

Although the emperor possessed the most prestigious of all lay titles, the actual authority of his office was very limited. Both the Habsburgs and their rivals used the office to promote their dynastic self-interests until the Habsburg line ascended the throne permanently with the reign of Frederick III (1442–93), the last emperor to be crowned in Rome. The imperial office and title were abolished when Napoleon dissolved the Holy Roman Empire in 1806.

THE CONSEQUENCES OF REFORM

The conflicts between emperors and popes constituted one conspicuous result of the reform movement. The transformation and new institutionalization of learning, the reconstitution of the church, the intensification of ecclesiastical discipline, and the growth of territorial monarchies were four others. Each of these developments was supported by the agricultural, technological, and commercial expansion of the 10th and 11th centuries.

THE TRANSFORMATION OF THOUGHT AND LEARNING

The polemics of the papal-imperial debate revealed the importance of establishing a set of canonical texts on the basis of which both sides could argue. A number of academic disciplines, particularly the study of dialectic, had developed considerably between the 9th and 12th centuries. By the 12th century it had become the most widely studied intellectual discipline, in part because it was an effective tool for constructing and refuting arguments. The Gregorian reformers had also based their arguments on canon law, and a number of Gregorian and post-Gregorian collections, particularly that of Ivo of Chartres (*c.* 1040–1116), pointed the way toward the creation of a commonly accessible canon law. That goal was achieved in about 1140–50 in two successive recensions (perhaps by two different authors) of a lawbook called *Concordia discordantium canonum* ("Concordance of Discordant Canons"), or *Decretum*, attributed to Master Gratian. The *Decretum* became the standard introductory text of ecclesiastical law. Simultaneously, the full text of the 6th-century body of Roman law, later called the *Corpus Iuris Civilis* ("Body of Civil Law"), began to circulate in northern Italy and was taught in the schools of Bologna. The learned character of the revived Roman law contributed powerfully to the development of legal science throughout Europe in the following centuries.

Early in the 12th century, Hugh of Saint-Victor (1096–1141), schoolmaster of a house of canons just outside Paris, wrote a description of all the subjects of learning, the *Didascalicon*. Hugh's contemporary, Peter Abelard (1079–1142), taught dialectic at Paris to crowds of students, many of whom became high officials in ecclesiastical and secular institutions. The teaching methods of scholars such as Gratian, Hugh, Abelard, and others became the foundation of Scholasticism, the method used by the new schools in the teaching of arts, law, medicine, and theology. In theology itself, comparable canonical work was done by Peter Lombard (*c.* 1100–60) in his *Sententiarum libri iv* ("Four

Peter Abelard with his wife, Héloïse, miniature portrait by Jean de Meun, 14th century; in the Musée Condé, Chantilly, France. Courtesy of the Musée Condé, Chantilly, Fr.; photograph, Giraudon/Art Resource, New York

Books of Sentences"), which became, next to the Bible, the fundamental teaching text of theology.

But not all Christians admired the new Scholastic theology. The Scholastic teaching of Scripture replaced the early contemplative monastic style of exegesis with dialectical investigative techniques and speculative theology. Many monks and some outraged laity thought that Scripture was being mishandled, stripped of its dignity and mystery in the service of feeble human logic and cold rationality. They did not, however, stop the tide, as Scholastic theology created a complex, effective, and highly persuasive means of discussing both the complexities of divinity and the moral obligations of Christians on earth.

As groups of teachers organized themselves into guilds in the late 12th and early 13th centuries, they and their students received imperial, papal, and royal privileges. About

1200 of these associations, modeling themselves on ecclesiastical corporations, developed into the first universities.
During the remainder of the 13th century, clerical teaching authority within the universities was articulated. The
first guilds were formed for the teaching of law at several
schools in Bologna and for the teaching of arts and theology at Paris and later at Oxford, Cambridge, and other
towns. With the foundation of the University of Prague in
1348, the model crossed the Rhine River for the first time.
By the 15th century it had become a standard fixture of
European learning.

University teachers insisted on the right to define
teaching authority. Proclaiming the earliest version of
academic freedom, they rejected outside interference and
asserted that their professional competence alone enti-
tled them to determine the content of disciplines and the
standards for admitting, examining, graduating, and cer-
tifying students. They also transformed both the written
script and the nature of the material book. Since teaching
required a readable script and books whose texts were as
close to identical as possible, the distinctive "Gothic" or
"black letter" script was developed, which standardized
abbreviations and the writing style used in texts.

The presence of universities of teachers and students
in western European society was significant in itself. The
universities reflected favourably on the cities in which
they were located and on the rulers who protected them.
The rulers also benefited from the opportunity to recruit
increasingly educated public servants and bureaucrats
from these institutions. The church benefited too, since
the universities produced theologians, canon lawyers, and
other officials that the church—even the papal office—
now seemed to require.

The universities aided in the recovery and dissemination of Aristotelianism, particularly in the physical sciences

and metaphysics. Only the new universities, moreover, could have housed and spread the intellectual work of Thomas Aquinas (1224/25–1274) and Bonaventure (1217–74), the greatest theologians of the 13th century, and of Henry of Segusio (Hostiensis; *c.* 1200–71) and Sinibaldo Fieschi (later Pope Innocent IV, reigned 1243–54), the greatest canon lawyers of the century.

ECCLESIASTICAL ORGANIZATION

With the removal of the most offensive instances of lay influence in ecclesiastical affairs, the organization of the universal church and local churches acquired a symmetry and consistency hardly possible before 1100. An 11th-century anonymous text that was accepted by canon law

St. Thomas Aquinas Enthroned Between the Doctors of the Old and New Testaments, with Personifications of the Virtues, Sciences, and Liberal Arts, *fresco by Andrea da Firenze, c. 1365; in the Spanish Chapel of the church of Santa Maria Novella, Florence.* SCALA/ Art Resource, New York

identified two orders of Christians, the clergy and the laity. It considered the clergy largely in a monastic context, indicating that the new attention to the secular clergy had transferred to them the virtues and discipline of monks. Although many monks were not ordained priests, their disciplined, contemplative life was held up for centuries as the ideal clerical model.

The work of the laity was the business of the world. The clergy, however, considered itself far more important than the laity. Members of the clergy themselves were ranked in terms of sacramental orders, minor and major. When a boy or young man entered the clergy, he received the tonsure, symbolizing his new status. He might then move in stages through the minor orders: acolyte, exorcist, lector, and doorkeeper. At the highest of minor orders the candidate could still leave the clergy. Many clerics in minor orders served in the administration of secular and ecclesiastical institutions. They also sometimes caused trouble in secular society, since even they received benefit of clergy, or exemption from trial in secular courts. Ordination to the major orders—subdeacon (elevated to a major order by Pope Innocent III in 1215), deacon, and priest—entailed vows of chastity and conferred sacramental powers on the recipient.

At the head of the Latin Christian church was the pope, whose powers were now articulated in canon law, most of which was made by the popes themselves and by their legal advisers. Not only did popes claim powers over even secular rulers in many instances, but a number of rulers, including King John of England (reigned 1199–1216), submitted their kingdoms to the popes and received them back to govern for their new spiritual and temporal masters. The popes also issued charters of foundation for universities, convened church councils, called Crusades and commissioned preachers to deliver Crusade sermons, and appointed papal judges delegate or subdelegate to investigate specific problems. In all these areas, as in the articulation of canon law, papal authority directly affected the lives of all Christians, as well as the lives of Jews and Muslims in their relations with Christians.

The popes were assisted by the College of Cardinals, which was transformed during the papal-imperial conflict from a group of Roman liturgical assistants into a body of advisers individually appointed by the popes. Among its duties articulated in conciliar and papal decrees of 1059 and 1179—rules still in effect in the Roman Catholic Church today—was to elect the pope. A cardinal could be a cardinal bishop (if the church he was given was outside the city of Rome, whose only bishop, of course, was the pope himself), a cardinal priest, or a cardinal deacon. Cardinals also had different roles. The cardinal bishop of Ostia, for example, always crowned a new pope. For some time the senior cardinal deacon gave the pope his papal name, a practice that began in the 10th century, perhaps in imitation of monastic tradition.

The papacy developed other means to implement its authority. After the Concordat of Worms (1122), which settled some aspects of the Investiture Controversy, popes held regular assemblies of higher clergy in church councils, the first of which was the first Lateran Council in 1123. Conciliar legislation was the means by which reform principles were most efficiently formulated and disseminated to the highest clerical levels. Although councils in the 12th, 13th, and 14th centuries were closely controlled by the popes, later councils sometimes opposed papal authority with claims to conciliar authority, a position generally known as conciliarism. Papal legates, judges, and emissaries, widely used by Gregory VII and later popes, were dispatched with full papal authority to deal with issues in distant parts of Europe.

Papal collectors, who received funds owed to the popes for Crusading or other purposes, were also essential components of papal government. The papal chamberlain of Celestine III (1191–98), Cencio Savelli (later Pope Honorius III; 1216–27), produced the *Liber Censuum* ("The Book of the Census") in 1192, the first comprehensive account of the sources of papal funding. In this respect, as in the formal communications of the papal chancery, the pope created an influential model, imitated by all other European principalities and kingdoms. Although only four papal registers (collections of important papal letters and decisions) from before 1198 survive more or less intact, all registers since then have been preserved.

The day-to-day work of the popes was carried out by the Roman Curia; the name Curia Romana was first used by Urban II at the end of the 11th century. The Curia consisted of the chancery; the Apostolic Camera, or financial centre; the consistory, or legal office, including the Roman Rota (chief papal court); and the Penitentiary, or spiritual and confessional office. The popes were also the secular rulers of Rome and the Papal States, and accordingly their servants included the rulers and officials of these territories.

The popes ran afoul of local movements for greater independence, including the revolution led by Arnold of Brescia, the priest and religious dissident, in 1143. Revolts continued throughout the 13th century and increased in frequency during the Avignon papacy (1305–78), when the popes resided in Avignon, and during the Great Schism (1378–1417), when there were two and then three claimants for the papal office. (The crisis was resolved in 1415–18 at the Council of Constance, which elected a new pope and restored papal authority over the city of Rome and the Papal States.) When a pope could safely reside in Rome, he worked at the church of St. John Lateran, his cathedral as bishop of the city of Rome, and not at the Vatican, which was chiefly a pilgrimage shrine. Only after Martin V (1417–31), the pope elected at the Council of Constance, found that the papal quarters at the Lateran had fallen into ruins was the papal residence and administration moved to the Vatican.

Lower levels of the clerical hierarchy replicated the papal administration on a smaller scale. The immense dioceses of northern Europe, ruled by prince-archbishops (as in Cologne) or by prince-bishops (as in Durham), were very different from the tiny rural dioceses of southern Italy. Within the secular clergy the highest rank below the pope was that of primate, who was usually the regional head of a group of archbishops. The archbishops, or metropolitans, ruled archdioceses, or provinces, holding provincial synods of clergy under their jurisdiction, ruling administrative courts, and supervising the suffragan bishops (bishops assigned to assist in the administration of the archdiocese). The archbishop was expected to make regular visits to the ecclesiastical institutions in his province and to hear appeals from the verdicts of courts at lower levels.

The archdiocese was divided into dioceses, each ruled by a bishop, who supervised his own administration and episcopal court. In ecclesiastical tradition, bishops were considered the successors of the Apostles, and a strong sense of episcopal collegiality between pope and bishops survived well into the age of increased papal authority. Episcopal courts included a chancery for the use of the bishop's seal, a judicial court under the direction of the official or the archdeacon, financial officers, and archpriests (priests assigned to special functions). The bishop's church, the cathedral, was staffed by a chapter (a body of clergy) and headed by a dean, who was specifically charged with administering the cathedral and its property. The chapter was not usually the bishop's administrative staff and thus sometimes found itself in conflict with the bishop. Struggles between bishop and chapter were frequent and notorious in canon law courts, since they could be appealed, like disputed episcopal elections, all the way to the papal court.

Episcopal powers were extensive: only the bishop could consecrate churches, ordain clergy, license preachers, or appoint teachers in episcopal schools. The bishop's pastoral responsibilities extended to all Christians in his diocese. Moreover, since canon law touched the lives of all Christians, episcopal legal officials held great power. They visited diocesan institutions and presided over trials of those accused of violating canon law, which concerned many areas that in modern legal systems are subsumed under civil and criminal law, family courts, and moral offenses.

The diocese was divided into deaconries for the archdeacons, which might convoke lesser synods. Deaconries too had their own chancellors, notaries, and judicial officers, as well as archpriests who assisted the deacons. Since the archdeacon or official was usually the point of contact between the laity and ecclesiastical discipline, they were often the butt of satire and complaint. One topic said to have been proposed for debate at a 13th-century university was: Can an archdeacon be saved?

At the lowest level of the clerical hierarchy was the parish, with its priest, suffragan priests, vicars, and chaplains, who together supervised the spiritual life of the majority of European laity. The parish owned its church and the land that provided the priest's income (the glebe). Additional income was derived from tithes collected from all parishioners and often from an endowment. The priest was presented to the bishop for ordination by a layman, cleric, or clerical corporation with proprietary rights over the parish. In many cases, the actual care of souls in a parish was in the hands of a vicar, who was deputed by a patron to perform the priest's duties when the priest was away studying or occupied in other business. The parish priest also administered the ecclesiastical calendar for his parishioners. Parishioners themselves might belong to spiritual associations, called confraternities, but all were expected to be baptized, to make confession once a year (after the fourth Lateran Council prescribed this in 1215), to take Holy Communion, to marry, and to be buried in the parish churchyard. The parish was the level at which most people learned their Christianity and the level at which most of them lived it.

DEVOTIONAL LIFE

The popes also supervised the regular clergy, which included the religious orders of monks, canons regular (secular clergy who lived collegiately according to a rule), and mendicants. Each of these orders had a superior, who was advised by a chapter general that comprised representatives of the religious houses of the order. Orders, like dioceses, were organized according to regions, each having a regional superior and holding regional chapters. Individual religious houses were headed by an abbot or abbess (the mendicant orders had a slightly different organization) and administered by a chancellor and chamberlain. Provosts and deans usually supervised the property of each house.

In the 12th century, new devotional movements (movements devoted to Jesus or the saints) led to outbursts of religious dissent (with new forms of ecclesiastical discipline devised to control them) and equally passionate expressions of orthodox devotion. Although monasticism was by then an old institution, one of the great themes of the century was the search for the apostolic life as monks, canons, and laypeople might live it. The canons regular were one result of this movement, as were new monastic orders, particularly the Cistercian Order. But the most dynamic movement was that of the mendicant orders, the Dominicans and the Franciscans, founded in the early 13th century.

The Order of Friars Minor, founded by the layman Francis of Assisi (1181/82–1226) to minister to the spiritual needs of the cities, spread widely and rapidly, as did the Order of Preachers, founded by the canon of Osma, Dominic of Guzmán (c. 1170–1221). These and other devotional movements of laypeople were supported by Pope Innocent III and his successors. The mendicant orders greatly influenced popular piety, because they specialized in preaching in new churches that were built to hold large crowds. Indeed, during this time the sermon came into its own as the most effective mass medium in Europe. The mendicants also increased devotion to the Virgin Mary and to the infant or crucified and suffering Jesus, rather than to the figure of Jesus as regal and remote.

Other forms of devotional life took shape during the 12th, 13th, and 14th centuries. The Cistercian Order, for example, instituted the status of lay brother, who was usually an adult layman who retired from the world to undertake the management of monastic resources. Still other members of the laity retired to the sequestered life of hermits and recluses, usually under the supervision of a chaplain.

During the 13th and 14th centuries, devotional movements arose that were neither monastic nor clerical in any other sense. The most notable of these was the Beguines, an order of devout women (and occasionally, but more rarely, men, who lived in all-male communities and were called Beghards) who lived together in devotional communities within towns, especially in the Low Countries and the Rhineland, followed no rule, and took no vow. They worked in the towns but lived collectively and might leave

St. Francis of Assisi, detail of a fresco by Cimabue, late 13th century; in the lower church of San Francesco, Assisi, Italy. Alinari—Anderson/Art Resource, New York

for marriage or another form of life at any time. Some of the most important devotional literature of the period was written by and for Beguines.

The vast movements of reform, ecclesiastical organization, and pastoral care of the 12th and 13th centuries reached their greatest intensity in the pontificate of Innocent III (1198–1216). Lothar of Segni, as he was originally known, was the son of a landholding noble family outside Rome. He was educated in the schools of Paris and attached to the Roman Curia in 1187. Innocent issued the strongest and most tightly argued claims for papal authority, and he launched Crusades and instituted the office of papal judge-delegate to combat clerical crimes and heterodox belief. He also supported the new mendicant orders, paid particular attention to the needs of popular devotion, reformed and disciplined the Curia, and assembled the fourth Lateran Council in November 1215. Innocent came as close to realizing the ideals of reform and renewal in ecclesiological practice as any pope before or since.

The organization of normative religion, the formal rules and norms of practice in the faith, was intended to give regularity and order to lived religion. Daily religious life was characterized by the acceptance of tradition and authority and by belief in the saints as patrons of local communities and belief in the parish priest as a conveyor of grace by virtue of his sacramental powers (conferred by ordination) and his legal powers (conferred by the bishop). During the 12th century, institutional structures for official acts of canonization were established, but the enthusiasm for the saints remained an important part of both popular devotion and the official cult of the saints (the system of religious belief and ritual surrounding the saints). The cult of the saints was celebrated by clergy and laity in the observance of feast days and processions, the veneration of saints' relics, pilgrimages to saints' shrines, and the rituals of death and burial near the graves of saints. The liturgical dimension of pastoral care regulated the major events of the day, week, season, and Christian year, according to whose rhythms everyone lived. Priests blessed harvests, animals, and ships and liturgically interceded in the face of natural or man-made disasters.

Religious devotion strengthened the presence of normative religion in marriage and the family, the sacred character of the local community and the territorial monarchy, and the moral rules by which lay affairs were conducted. The fourth Lateran Council largely institutionalized the work of the 12th-century moral theologians at Paris, who had begun to apply the principles of doctrine and canon law to the lives of their contemporaries.

THE EMERGENCE OF A NEW ECCLESIASTICAL DISCIPLINE

The ecclesiastical reform movements that sharply distinguished clergy from laity also developed a means of sustaining that distinction through intensified ecclesiastical discipline. Clergy were not only freed from most forms of subordination to laypersons but also were granted legal privileges, being triable only in church courts and subject only to penalties deemed suitable by church authorities (benefit of clergy). Laity who injured clerical personnel or property were punished more harshly. But the distinction between clergy and laity also enhanced lay status. Lay authorities could legally perform judicial actions that were forbidden to clergy, like the shedding of blood or other forms of physical punishment. Clerical thinkers greatly legitimated lay activities that earlier monastic Christianity had once scorned, attributing a positive value to commerce, the law, just warfare, marriage, and other roles once considered signs of fallen and weak human nature.

The intensity of the reform movements led to a new
and elaborated idea of sin and to categories of sin so grave
that they required the harshest punishments, sometimes
in cooperation with lay courts. The idea of crime itself,
drawing on both older Roman law and earlier ecclesiastical discipline, gradually came to assume a distinctive place
in secular law, as more and more conflicts that had once
been settled privately came within the purview of lay legal
officials. Clerical crime became a major focus of disciplinary concern. The term *heresy*, loosely used until the 11th
century, slowly became better defined and was initially
applied to clerical misconduct such as simony (the acceptance of ecclesiastical office from laymen) and nicolaitism
(clerical marriage). The increasingly precise exposition of
Christian doctrine by 12th-century theologians seemed to
many people a displacement of the Christianity that they
had always understood and practiced. Legal collections
began to treat various forms of doctrinal and devotional
dissent as heresy, thus formulating a category that would
criminalize a wide variety of beliefs and conduct.

Promoters of the new ecclesiastical doctrine and discipline believed that the increasingly numerous devotional
collectives and their charismatic leaders would eventually threaten the order of both clerical and lay society.
In the early 13th century the English theologian Robert
Grosseteste formulated a definition that accurately
reflected the changed understanding of religious dissent:
"Heresy is an opinion chosen by human faculties, contrary
to sacred scripture, openly taught, and pertinaciously
defended." Criminal heresy involved belief that contradicted orthodox doctrine and was arrived at by purely
human capacities. It was also belief that was publicly, and
therefore seditiously, proclaimed, even after legitimate
instruction by authorized teachers, thereby making the
"heretic" contumacious in the eyes of the law.

Like the problem of criminal clergy, the problem of heresy raised procedural questions in law. Legal procedure in criminal cases might be initiated by an accusation by a responsible individual or by a denunciation by a group of specially appointed synodal witnesses. In 1199 Innocent III added a third procedure, that of inquisition, or inquiry by an appropriate authority, which was first used to investigate clerical crimes. Later popes appointed judges delegate as individual inquisitors, although there was not an institutionalized office of inquisition until the royal-papal establishment of the Spanish Inquisition in 1478.

CHRISTIANITY, JUDAISM, AND ISLAM

The sacred texts of revealed religions may be eternal and unchanging, but they are understood and applied by human beings living in time. Christians believed not only that the Jews had misunderstood Scripture, thus justifying the Christian reinterpretation of Jewish Scripture, but that all of Jewish Scripture had to be understood as containing only partial truth. The whole truth was comprehensible only when Jewish Scripture was interpreted correctly, in what Christians called a "spiritual" rather than merely a "carnal" manner.

Although early Christian texts and later papal commands had prohibited the persecution and forced conversion of Jews, these doctrines were less carefully observed starting in the 11th century. Heralded by a series of pogroms in both Europe and the Middle East carried out in the course of the First Crusade, a deeper and more widespread anti-Judaism came to characterize much of European history after 1100. There also emerged in this period what some historians have termed "chimeric" anti-Judaism, the conception of the Jew not only as ignorant of spiritual truth and stubbornly resistant to Christian preaching but as actively hostile to Christianity and guilty of ugly crimes against it, such as the ritual murder of Christian children and the desecration of the consecrated host of the mass. This form of anti-Judaism resulted in massacres of Jews, usually at moments of high social tension within Christian communities. One of the best documented of these massacres took place at York, Eng., in 1190.

Before the 11th century the Jews faced little persecution, lived among Christians, and even pursued the same occupations as Christians. The Jews' restricted status after that time encouraged many of them to turn to moneylending, which only served to increase Christian hostility (Christians were forbidden to lend money to other Christians). Because the Jews often undertook on behalf of rulers work that Christians would not do or were not encouraged to do, such as serving as physicians and financial officers, Jews were hated both for their religion and for their social roles.

Jewish identity was also visually marked. Jews were depicted in particular ways in art, and the fourth Lateran Council in 1215 insisted that Jews wear identifying marks on their clothing. Even when not savagely persecuted, Jews were considered the property of the territorial monarchs of Europe and could be routinely exploited economically and even expelled, as they were from England in 1290, France in 1306, and Spain in 1492.

Yet Christians also believed that it was necessary for the Jews to continue to exist unconverted, because the Apocalypse, or Revelation to John, the last book of the Christian Bible, stated that the Jews would be converted at the end of time. Therefore, a "saving remnant" of Jews needed to exist so that scriptural prophecy would be fulfilled.

Muslims, on the other hand, possessed neither the historical status of Jews nor their place in salvation history (the course of events from Creation to the Last

Judgment). To many Christian thinkers, Muslims were former Christian heretics who worshipped Muhammad, the Prophet of Islam, and were guilty of occupying the Holy Land and threatening Christendom with military force. The First Crusade had been launched to liberate the Holy Land from Islamic rule, and later Crusades were undertaken to defend the original conquest.

The Crusading movement failed for many reasons but mainly because the material requirements for sustaining a military and political outpost so far from the heartland of western Europe were not met. But as a component of European culture, the Crusade ideal remained prominent, even in the 15th and 16th centuries, when the powerful Ottoman Empire indeed threatened to sweep over Mediterranean and southeastern Europe. Not until the Treaty of Carlowitz in 1699 was a stable frontier between the Ottoman Empire and the Holy Roman Empire established.

Contempt for Islam and fear of Muslim military power did not, however, prevent a lively and expansive commercial and technological transfer between the two civilizations or between them and the Byzantine Empire. Commercial and intellectual exchanges between Islamic lands and western Europe were considerable. Muslim maritime, agricultural, and technological innovations, as well as much East Asian technology via the Muslim world, made their way to western Europe in one of the largest technology transfers in world history. What Europeans did not invent they readily borrowed and adapted for their own use. Of the three great civilizations of western Eurasia and North Africa, that of Christian Europe began as the least developed in virtually all aspects of material and intellectual culture, well behind the Islamic states and Byzantium. By the end of the 13th century it had begun to pull even, and by the end of the 15th century it had surpassed both. The late 15th-century voyages of discovery were not something new but a more ambitious continuation of the European interest in distant parts of the world.

FROM TERRITORIAL PRINCIPALITIES TO TERRITORIAL MONARCHIES

As a result of the Investiture Controversy of the late 11th and early 12th centuries, the office of emperor lost much of its religious character and retained only a nominal universal preeminence over other rulers, though several 12th- and 13th-century emperors reasserted their authority on the basis of their interpretation of Roman law and energetically applied their lordship and pursued their dynastic interests in Germany and northern Italy. But the struggle over investiture and the reform movement also legitimized all secular authorities, partly on the grounds of their obligation to enforce discipline. The most successful rulers of the 12th and 13th centuries were, first, individual lords who created compact and more intensely governed principalities and, second and most important and enduring, kings who successfully asserted their authority over the princes, often with princely cooperation. The monarchies of England, France, León-Castile, Aragon, Scandinavia, Portugal, and elsewhere all acquired their fundamental shape and character in the 12th century.

THE OFFICE AND PERSON OF THE KING

By the 12th century, most European political thinkers agreed that monarchy was the ideal form of governance, since it imitated on earth the model set by God for the universe. It was also the form of government of the ancient Hebrews, the Roman Empire, and the peoples who succeeded Rome after the 4th century. For several centuries,

Crusades

The Crusades were a series of military expeditions, beginning in the late 11th century, that were organized by Western Christians in response to centuries of Muslim wars of expansion. Their objectives were to check the spread of Islam, to retake control of the Holy Land, to conquer pagan areas, and to recapture formerly Christian territories. They were seen by many of their participants as a means of redemption and expiation for sins. Between 1095, when the First Crusade was launched, and 1291, when the Latin Christians were finally expelled from their kingdom in Syria, there were numerous expeditions to the Holy Land, to Spain, and even to the Baltic. The Crusades continued for several centuries after 1291, usually as military campaigns intended to halt or slow the advance of Muslim power or to conquer pagan areas. Crusading declined rapidly during the 16th century with the advent of the Protestant Reformation and the decline of papal authority. The Crusades constitute a controversial chapter in the history of Christianity, and their excesses have been the subject of centuries of historiography.

some areas had no monarch, but these were regarded as anomalies. Iceland (until its absorption by Norway in 1262) was governed by an association of free men and heads of households meeting in an annual assembly. Many city-republics in northern Italy—especially Florence, Milan, Genoa, Pisa, and Venice—were in effect independent from the 10th to the 16th century, though they were nominally under the rule of the emperor. Elsewhere in Europe, the prosperous and volatile cities of the Low Countries frequently asserted considerable independence from the counts of Flanders and the dukes of Brabant. In the 15th century the forest cantons of Switzerland won effective independence from their episcopal and lay masters. For the rest of Europe, however, monarchy was both a theoretical norm and a factual reality.

Whereas kings were originally rulers of peoples, from the 11th century they gradually became rulers of peoples in geographic territories, and kingdoms came to designate both ruled peoples and the lands they inhabited. Gradually, inventories of royal resources, royal legislation, and the idea of borders and territorial maps became components of territorial monarchies.

Kings acquired their thrones by inheritance, by election or acclamation (as in the empire), or by conquest. The first two means were considered the most legitimate, unless conquest was carried out at the request or command of a legitimate authority, usually the pope. The king's position was confirmed by a coronation ceremony, which acknowledged what royal blood claimed: a dynastic right to the throne, borne by a family rather than a designated individual. Inheritance of the throne might involve the successor's being designated coruler while the previous king still lived (as in France), designation by the will of the predecessor, or simply agreement and acclamation by the most important and powerful royal subjects. When dynasties died out in the male line, the search for a ruler became more complicated; when they died out in the male line and a woman succeeded, there were usually intense debates about the legitimacy of female succession. Liturgical anointing with consecrated oil was accompanied by the ceremonial presentation to the king of objects with symbolic meaning (the crown, the sword of justice, and the helmet, robe, and scepter), by the chanting of prayers dedicated to rulership, and usually by an oath, in which the king swore to protect the church, the weak, and the peace of his kingdom, to administer justice, and to defend the kingdom against its (and his) enemies.

From the very beginning of European history, kings had responsibilities as well as rights and powers. Kings who were thought to have violated their oaths might be considered tyrants or incompetents, and a number of kings were deposed by local factions or papal command, especially in the 13th and 14th centuries. Depositions also required ceremonies that reversed the coronation liturgy.

INSTRUMENTS OF ROYAL GOVERNANCE

Kings ruled through their courts, which were gradually transformed from private households into elaborate bureaucracies. Royal religious needs were served by royal chapels—whose personnel often became bishops in the kingdom—and by clerical chancellors, who were responsible for issuing and sealing royal documents. Royal chanceries, financial offices, and law courts became specialized institutions during the 12th century. They recruited people of skill as well as of respectable birth, and they established programs to ensure uniformity and norms of professional competence, goals that were increasingly aided by the education offered by the new universities.

In some circumstances, kings were expected to seek and follow the advice of the most important men in their kingdoms, and these gatherings were formalized after the 12th century. Kings also sometimes convened larger assemblies of lower-ranking subjects in order to issue their commands or urge approval of financial demands. As kings grew stronger and their bureaucracies more articulated, their costs, particularly for war, also increased. Greater financial needs often determined a king's use of representative institutions in order to gain widespread acceptance of new direct or indirect taxation.

These assemblies developed differently in different kingdoms. In England the first Parliaments were held in the late 13th century, though they were not powerful institutions until the 16th century. In France the Parlement developed into a royal law court, while the intermittent meetings of the Estates-General (a representative assembly of the three orders of society) served as an instrument of consultation and communication for the kings. Across Europe these representative assemblies were composed differently, functioned differently, and possessed different degrees of influence on the ruler and the rest of the kingdom. Their later role as essential and powerful components of government began only in the 16th and 17th centuries.

The territorial monarchies represented something entirely new in world history. Although they often borrowed from the political literature of antiquity——from the Greek philosopher Aristotle, the Roman statesman Cicero, and Roman epic poetry—they applied it to a very different world, one whose ideas were shaped by courtiers, professors, and canon lawyers as well as by political philosophers. Incorporating both clergy and laity under vigorous royal dynasties, the kingdoms of Europe grew out of the political experience of the papacy, the north Italian city-republics, and their own internal development. By the 15th century the territorial monarchies had laid the groundwork for the modern state. When, to further their own interests, they began to incorporate successively lower levels of society, they also laid the groundwork for the nation. The combination of these, the nation-state, became the characteristic form of the early modern European and Atlantic polity.

THE THREE ORDERS

In the 11th and 12th centuries thinkers argued that human society consisted of three orders: those who fight, those who pray, and those who labour. The structure of the second order, the clergy, was in place by 1200 and remained intact until the religious reformations of the 16th century. The very general category of those who labour (specifically, those who were not knightly warriors or nobles) diversified rapidly after the 11th century into the lively and energetic worlds of peasants, skilled artisans, merchants, financiers, lay professionals, and entrepreneurs, which together drove the European economy to its greatest achievements. The first order, those who fight, was the rank of the politically powerful, ambitious, and dangerous. Kings took pains to ensure that it did not resist their authority.

The term *noble* was originally used to refer to members of kinship groups whose names and heroic past were known, respected, and recognized by others (though it was not usually used by members of such groups themselves). Noble groups married into each other, recognizing the importance of both the female and the male lines. Charlemagne used this international nobility to rule his empire, and its descendants became the nobility of the 11th and 12th centuries, though by then the understanding of noble status had changed. During the 11th century, however, some branches of these broad groups began to identify themselves increasingly with the paternal line and based their identity on their possession of a particular territory handed down from generation to generation, forming patriarchal lineages whose consciousness of themselves differed from that of their predecessors. Titles such as count or duke were originally those of royal service and might increase the prestige and wealth of a family but were not originally essential to noble status. Nor were even kings thought to be able to ennoble someone who was not noble by birth. As the status of the free peasant population was diminished, freedom and unfreedom gradually became the most significant social division.

The new warrior order encompassed both great nobles and lesser fighting men who depended upon the great nobles for support. This assistance usually took the form of land or income drawn from the lord's resources, which could also bring the hope of social advancement, even marriage into a lordly family. The acute need on the part of these lower-ranking warriors was to distinguish themselves from peasants—hence the relegation of all who were not warriors to the vague category of those who labour.

Some nobles asserted their nobility by seizing territory, controlling it and its inhabitants from a castle, surviving as local powers over several generations, marrying well, achieving recognition from their neighbours, and dispensing ecclesiastical patronage to nearby monasteries. The greatest and wealthiest of the nobles controlled vast areas of land, which they received by inheritance or through a grant from the king. Some of them developed closely governed territorial principalities which, in France, were eventually absorbed and redistributed by the crown to members of the royal family or their favourites. Despite the extreme diversity between knights, lesser nobility, and greater nobility, their common warrior-culture, expressed in the literature and ideology of chivalry, served as an effective social bond, excluding all those who did not share it.

As the territorial monarchies gradually increased in both prestige and power, the higher nobility adjusted by accepting more royal offices, titles, and patronage, developing an elaborate vocabulary of noble status, and restricting access to its ranks even though kings could now ennoble whomever they chose. The culture of chivalry served the ambitions of the lower-ranking nobility, but it also reflected the spectrum of different levels of nobility, all subordinated to the ruler. The culture and power of the European aristocracy lasted until the end of the 18th century.

CRISIS, RECOVERY, AND RESILIENCE

Both ancient and modern historians have often conceived the existence of civilizations and historical periods in terms of the biological stages of human life: birth, development, maturity, and decay. Once the Middle Ages was identified as a distinct historical period, historians in the 15th and 16th centuries began to describe it as enduring in a sequence of stages from youthful vigour to maturity (in the 12th and 13th centuries) and then sinking into old age (in the 14th and 15th centuries). Much of the evidence used to support this view was based on the series of apparently great disasters that struck Europe in the 14th century: the Mongol invasions, the great famine of 1315, the Black Death of 1348 and subsequent years, the financial collapse of the great Italian banking houses in the early 14th century, and the vastly increased costs and devastating effects of larger-scale warfare. For a long time historians considered these disasters dramatic signs of the end of an age, especially because they already believed that the Renaissance had emerged following the collapse of medieval civilization.

Reconsideration of the Europe of the 14th and 15th centuries, however, does not reveal decline or decay but rather a remarkable resilience that enabled it to recover from disaster and reconstitute itself by means of most of the same institutions it had possessed in 1300. Only from a highly selective and partial historical perspective was there ever, as the great Dutch historian Johan Huizinga once termed it, a "waning," "autumn," or "end" of the Middle Ages.

The process of rural and urban expansion and development indeed paused in the 14th century as famine, epidemic disease, intensified and prolonged warfare, and financial collapse brought growth to a halt and reduced

Mongol warriors, miniature from Rashīd al-Dīn's History of the World, *1307; in the Edinburgh University Library, Scotland.* Courtesy of the Edinburgh University Library, Scotland

the population for a time to about half of the 70 million people who had inhabited Europe in 1300. But the resources that had created the Europe of the 12th and 13th centuries survived these crises: first the European countryside and then the cities were rapidly repopulated. It is the resiliency of Europe, not its weakness, that explains the patterns of recovery in the late 14th and 15th centuries. That recovery continued through the 16th and 17th centuries.

The missionary mandate reached out across Mongol-dominated Asia as far east as China, where a Christian bishop took up his seat in 1307. The Mongol opening of Eurasia also relocated Europe in the minds of its inhabitants. No longer were its edges simply its borders with the Islamic world. Improved techniques in both navigation and marine engineering led Europeans from the 13th century to cross and map first their local seas, then the west African coasts, then the Atlantic and Pacific. From the late 15th century Europe began to export itself once more, as it once had to the north and east from the 10th to the 15th century, this time over vast oceans and to continents that had been unknown to the Greeks and Romans.

Neither the crises of the 14th century nor the voyages and discoveries of the 15th suggest the end of a historical period or an exhausted medieval Europe. The resilience and capacity for innovation of 14th- and 15th-century Europe, the hopeful, determined, and often passionate search for salvation on the part of ordinary people leading ordinary lives, even the inability of governments to weigh down their subjects without fierce displays of resistance — all indicate the strength of a European society and culture that men and women had shaped from the 8th century.

CHAPTER 5

THE RENAISSANCE

Few historians are comfortable with the triumphalist and western Europe-centred image of the Renaissance as the irresistible march of modernity and progress. A sharp break with medieval values and institutions, a new awareness of the individual, an awakened interest in the material world and nature, and a recovery of the cultural heritage of ancient Greece and Rome—these were once understood to be the major achievements of the Renaissance. Today, every particular of this formula is under suspicion if not altogether repudiated. Nevertheless, the term Renaissance remains a widely recognized label for the multifaceted period between the heyday of medieval universalism, as embodied in the papacy and Holy Roman Empire, and the convulsions and sweeping transformations of the 17th century.

In this period some important innovations of the Middle Ages came into their own, including the revival of urban life, commercial enterprise based on private capital, banking, the formation of states, systematic investigation of the physical world, Classical scholarship, and vernacular literatures. In religious life the Renaissance was a time of the broadening and institutionalizing of earlier initiatives in lay piety and lay-sponsored clerical reforms, rather than of the abandonment of traditional beliefs. In government, city-states and regional and national principalities supplanted the fading hegemony of the empire and the papacy and obliterated many of the local feudal jurisdictions that had covered Europe, although within states power continued to be monopolized by elites drawing their strength from both landed and mercantile wealth. If there was a Renaissance "rediscovery of the world and of man," as the 19th-century historians Jules Michelet (in the seventh volume of his *History of France*) and Jacob Burckhardt (in *The Civilization of the Renaissance in Italy* [1860]) asserted, it can be found mainly in literature and art, influenced by the latest and most successful of a long series of medieval Classical revivals. For all but exceptional individuals and a few marginal groups, the standards of behaviour continued to arise from traditional social and moral codes. Identity derived from class, family, occupation, and community, although each of these social forms was itself undergoing significant modification. Thus, for example, while there is no substance to Burckhardt's notion that in Italy women enjoyed perfect equality with men, the economic and structural features of Renaissance patrician families may have enhanced the scope of activity and influence of women of that class. Finally, the older view of the Renaissance centred too exclusively on Italy, and within Italy on a few cities—Florence, Venice, and Rome. By discarding false dichotomies—Renaissance versus Middle Ages, Classical versus Gothic, modern versus feudal—one is able to grasp more fully the interrelatedness of Italy with the rest of Europe and to investigate the extent to which the great centres of Renaissance learning and art were nourished and influenced by less exalted towns and by changes in the pattern of rural life.

THE ITALIAN RENAISSANCE

The Renaissance in Italy was marked by the flourishing of its city-states. Against a backdrop of civic strife and wars with their rivals, Italian cities fostered an intellectual movement called humanism. Italian humanists emphasized the importance of the Classical literature of the ancient Greeks and Romans, and they focused their interest on secular, rather than religious, topics. Their areas of study, which included language, literature, politics, and history, are known collectively as the humanities. Humanism achieved fruition first in northern Italy during the 13th and 14th centuries; it later spread through continental Europe and England, in what became known as the northern Renaissance.

URBAN GROWTH

Although town revival was a general feature of 10th- and 11th-century Europe (associated with an upsurge in population that is not completely understood), in Italy the urban imprint of Roman times had never been erased. By the 11th century, the towers of new towns, and, more commonly, of old towns newly revived, began to dot the spiny Italian landscape—eye-catching creations of a burgeoning population literally brimming with new energy due to improved diets. As in Roman times, the medieval Italian town lived in close relation to its surrounding rural area, or *contado*; Italian city folk seldom relinquished their ties to the land from which they and their families had sprung. Rare was the successful tradesman or banker who did not invest some of his profits in the family farm or a rural noble who did not spend part of the year in his house inside city walls.

In Italian towns, knights, merchants, rentiers, and skilled craftsmen lived and worked side by side, fought in the same militia, and married into each other's families. Social hierarchy existed, but it was a tangled system with no simple division between noble and commoner, between landed and commercial wealth. That landed magnates took part in civic affairs helps explain the early militancy of the townsfolk in resisting the local bishop, who was usually the principal claimant to lordship in the community.

Political action against a common enemy tended to infuse townspeople with a sense of community and civic loyalty. By the end of the 11th century, civic patriotism began to express itself in literature; city chronicles combined fact and legend to stress a city's Roman origins and, in some cases, its inheritance of Rome's special mission to rule. Such motifs reflect the cities' achievement of autonomy from their respective episcopal or secular feudal overlords and, probably, the growth of rivalries between neighbouring communities.

Rivalry between towns was part of the expansion into the neighbouring countryside, with the smaller and weaker towns submitting to the domination of the larger and stronger. As the activity of the towns became more complex, sporadic collective action was replaced by permanent civic institutions. Typically, the first of these was an executive magistracy, named the consulate (to stress the continuity with republican Rome). In the late 11th and early 12th centuries, this process—consisting of the establishment of juridical autonomy, the emergence of a permanent officialdom, and the spread of power beyond the walls of the city to the *contado* and neighbouring towns—was well under way in about a dozen Italian centres and evident in dozens more; the loose urban community was becoming a corporate entity, or commune; the city was becoming a city-state.

The typical 13th-century city-state was a republic administering a territory of dependent towns; whether it was a democracy is a question of definition. The idea of popular sovereignty existed in political thought and was reflected in the practice of calling a *parlamento*, or mass meeting, of the populace in times of emergency, but in none of the republics were the people as a whole admitted to regular participation in government. On the other hand, the 13th century saw the establishment, after considerable struggle, of assemblies in which some portion of the male citizenry, restricted by property and other qualifications, took part in debate, legislation, and the selection of officials. Most offices were filled by men serving on a rotating, short-term basis. If the almost universal obligation of service in the civic militia is also considered, it becomes clear that participation in the public life of the commune was shared by a considerable part of the male population, although the degree of participation varied from one commune to another and tended to decline. Most of the city republics were small enough (in 1300 Florence, one of the largest, had perhaps 100,000 people; Padua, nearer the average, had about 15,000) so that public business was conducted by and for citizens who knew each other, and civic issues were a matter of widespread and intense personal concern.

The darker side of this intense community life was conflict. It became a cliché of contemporary observers that when townsmen were not fighting their neighbours they were fighting each other. Machiavelli explained this as the result of the natural enmity between nobles and "the people—the former desiring to command, the latter unwilling to obey." This contains an essential truth: a basic problem was the unequal distribution of power and privilege, but the class division was further complicated by factional rivalry within the ruling groups and by ideological differences—Guelfism, or loyalty to the pope, versus Ghibellinism, or vassalage to the German emperors. The continuing leadership of the old knightly class, with its violent feudal ways and the persistence of a winner-take-all conception of politics, guaranteed bloody and devastating conflict. Losers could expect to be condemned to exile, with their houses burned and their property confiscated. Winners had to be forever vigilant against the unending conspiracies of exiles yearning to return to their homes and families.

During the 14th century a number of cities, despairing of finding a solution to the problem of civic strife, were turning from republicanism to *signoria*, the rule of one man. The *signore*, or lord, was usually a member of a local feudal family that was also a power in the commune. Thus, lordship did not appear to be an abnormal development, particularly if the *signore* chose, as most did, to rule through existing republican institutions. Sometimes a *signoria* was established as the result of one noble faction's victory over another, while in a few cases a feudal noble who had been hired by the republic as its *condottiere*, or military captain, became its master. Whatever the process, hereditary lordship had become the common condition and free republicanism the exception by the late 14th century. Contrary to what Burckhardt believed, Italy in the 14th century had not shaken off feudalism. In the south, feudalism was entrenched in the loosely centralized Kingdom of Naples, successor state to the Hohenstaufen and Norman kingdoms. In central and northern Italy, feudal lordship and knightly values merged with medieval communal institutions to produce the typical state of the Renaissance. Where the nobles were excluded by law from political participation in the commune, as in the Tuscan cities of Florence, Siena, Pisa, and Lucca, parliamentary republicanism had a longer life, but even these bastions of liberty had intervals of disguised or open lordship. The great maritime republic of Venice reversed the usual process by increasing the powers of its councils at the expense of the doge (from Latin *dux*, "leader"). However, Venice never had a feudal nobility, only a merchant aristocracy that called itself noble and jealously guarded its hereditary sovereignty against incursions from below.

WARS OF EXPANSION

There were new as well as traditional elements in the Renaissance city-state. Changes in the political and economic situation affected the evolution of government, while the growth of the humanist movement influenced developing conceptions of citizenship, patriotism, and civic history. The decline in the ability of both the empire and the papacy to dominate Italian affairs as they had done in the past left each state free to pursue its own goals within the limits of its resources. These goals were, invariably, the security and power of each state vis-à-vis its neighbours. Diplomacy became a skilled game of experts. Rivalries were deadly, and warfare was endemic.

Because the costs of war were all-consuming, particularly as mercenary troops replaced citizen militias, the states had to find new sources of revenue and develop methods of securing public credit. Governments borrowed from moneylenders (stimulating the development of banking), imposed customs duties, and levied fines; but, as their costs continued to exceed revenues, they came up with new solutions such as the forced loan, funded debt, and taxes on property and income. New officials with special skills were required to take property censuses (the *catasto*), calculate assessments, and manage budgets, as well as to provision troops, take minutes of council meetings, administer justice, write to other governments, and send instructions to envoys and other agents.

All this required public space—council, judicial, and secretarial rooms, storage space for bulging archives, and both closed and open-air ceremonial settings where officials interacted with the citizenry and received foreign visitors. As secular needs joined and blended with religious ones, towns took their place alongside the church and the monasteries as patrons of builders, painters, and sculptors (often the same persons). In the late 13th century, great programs of public building and decoration were begun that were intended to symbolize and portray images of civic power and beneficence and to communicate the values of "the common good." Thus the expansion of the functions of the city-state was accompanied by the development of a public ideology and a civic rhetoric intended to make people conscious of their blessings and responsibilities as citizens.

The city-state tended to subsume many of the protective and associative functions and loyalties connected with clan, family, guild, and party. Whether it fostered individualism by replacing traditional forms of association—as Burckhardt, Alfred von Martin, and other historians have claimed—is problematic. The Renaissance "discovery of the individual" is a nebulous concept, lending itself to many different meanings. It could be argued, for example, that the development of communal law, with its strong Roman influence, enhanced individual property rights or that participatory government promoted a consciousness of individual value. It could also be argued, however, that the city-state was a more effective controller of the loyalty and property of its members than were feudal jurisdictions and voluntary associations. In some respects the great merchants and bankers of the Renaissance, operating in international markets, had more freedom than local tradespeople, who were subject to guild restrictions, communal price and quality controls, and usury laws, but the economic ideal of Renaissance states was mercantilism, not free private enterprise.

Amid the confusion of medieval Italian politics, a new pattern of relations emerged by the 14th century. No longer revolving in the papal or in the imperial orbit, the stronger states were free to assert their hegemony over the weaker, and a system of regional power centres evolved.

From time to time the more ambitious states, especially those that had brought domestic conflict under control, made a bid for a wider hegemony in the peninsula, such as Milan attempted under the lordship of the Visconti family. In the 1380s and '90s Gian Galeazzo Visconti pushed Milanese power eastward as far as Padua, at the very doorstep of Venice, and southward to the Tuscan cities of Lucca, Pisa, and Siena and even to Perugia in papal territory. Some believed that Gian Galeazzo meant to be king of Italy; whether or not this is true, he would probably have overrun Florence, the last outpost of resistance in central Italy, had he not died suddenly in 1402, leaving a divided inheritance and much confusion. In the 1420s, under Filippo Maria, Milan began to expand again, but by then Venice, with territorial ambitions of its own, had joined with Florence to block Milan's advance, while the other Italian states took sides or remained neutral according to their own interests. The mid-15th century saw the Italian peninsula embroiled in a turmoil of intrigues, plots, revolts, wars, and shifting alliances, of which the most sensational was the reversal that brought the two old enemies, Florence and Milan, together against Venetian expansion. This "diplomatic revolution," supported by Cosimo de' Medici, the unofficial head of the Florentine republic, is the most significant illustration of the emergence of balance-of-power diplomacy in Renaissance Italy.

ITALIAN HUMANISM

The notion that ancient wisdom and eloquence lay slumbering in the Dark Ages until awakened in the Renaissance was the creation of the Renaissance itself. The idea of the revival of Classical antiquity is one of those great myths, comparable to the idea of the universal civilizing mission of imperial Rome or to the idea of progress in a modern industrial society, by which an era defines itself in history. Like all such myths, it is a blend of fact and invention. Classical thought and style permeated medieval culture in ways past counting. Most of the authors known to the Renaissance were known to the Middle Ages as well, while the Classical texts "discovered" by the humanists were often not originals but medieval copies preserved in monastic or cathedral libraries. Moreover, the Middle Ages had produced at least two earlier revivals of Classical antiquity. The so-called Carolingian Renaissance of the late 8th and 9th centuries saved many ancient works from destruction or oblivion, passing them down to posterity in its beautiful minuscule script (which influenced the humanist scripts of the Renaissance). A 12th-century Renaissance saw the revival of Roman law, Latin poetry, and Greek science, including almost the whole corpus of Aristotelian writings known today.

Visconti Castle in Pavia, Italy. Some historians speculate that Gian Galeazzo Visconti, ruler of Milan in the 14th century, had ambitions beyond his Milanese dominion to become king of Italy. W. Buss/De Agostini/ Getty Images

GROWTH OF LITERACY

Nevertheless, the Classical revival of the Italian Renaissance was so different from these earlier movements in spirit and substance that the humanists might justifiably claim that it was original and unique. During most of the Middle Ages, Classical studies and virtually all intellectual activities were carried on by churchmen, usually members of the monastic orders. In the Italian cities, this monopoly was partially breached by the growth of a literate laity with some taste and need for literary culture. New professions reflected the growth of both literary and specialized lay education—the *dictatores*, or teachers of practical rhetoric, lawyers, and the ever-present notary (a combination of solicitor and public recorder). These, and not Burckhardt's wandering scholar-clerics, were the true predecessors of the humanists.

In Padua a kind of early humanism emerged, flourished, and declined between the late 13th and early 14th centuries. Paduan Classicism was a product of the vigorous republican life of the commune, and its decline coincided with the loss of the city's liberty. A group of Paduan jurists, lawyers, and notaries—all trained as *dictatores*—developed a taste for Classical literature that probably stemmed from their professional interest in Roman law and their affinity for the history of the Roman Republic. The most famous of these Paduan Classicists was Albertino Mussato, a poet, historian, and playwright, as well as lawyer and politician, whose play *Ecerinis*, modeled on Seneca, has been called the first Renaissance tragedy. By reviving several types of ancient literary forms and by promoting the use of Classical models for poetry and rhetoric, the Paduan humanists helped make the 14th-century Italians more conscious of their Classical heritage; in other respects, however, they remained close to their medieval antecedents, showing little comprehension of the vast cultural and historical gulf that separated them from the ancients.

LANGUAGE AND ELOQUENCE

It was Francesco Petrarca, or Petrarch, who first understood fully that antiquity was a civilization apart and, understanding it, outlined a program of Classically oriented studies that would lay bare its spirit. The focus of Petrarch's insight was language: if Classical antiquity was to be understood in its own terms, it would be through the speech with which the ancients had communicated their thoughts. This meant that the languages of antiquity had to be studied as the ancients had used them and not as vehicles for carrying modern thoughts. Thus, grammar, which included the reading and careful imitation of ancient authors from a linguistic point of view, was the basis of Petrarch's entire program.

From the mastery of language, one moved on to the attainment of eloquence. For Petrarch, as for Cicero, eloquence was not merely the possession of an elegant style, nor yet the power of persuasion, but the union of elegance and power together with virtue. One who studied language and rhetoric in the tradition of the great orators of antiquity did so for a moral purpose—to persuade men and women to the good life—for, said Petrarch in a dictum that could stand as the slogan of Renaissance humanism, "it is better to will the good than to know the truth."

THE HUMANITIES

To will the good, one must first know it, and so there could be no true eloquence without wisdom. According to Leonardo Bruni, a leading humanist of the next generation, Petrarch "opened the way for us to show in what manner we might acquire learning." Petrarch's union of rhetoric and philosophy, modeled on the Classical ideal of eloquence, provided the humanists with an intellectual dignity and a moral ethos lacking to the medieval *dictatores* and Classicists. It also pointed the way toward a program of studies — the *studia humanitatis* — by which the ideal might be achieved.

As elaborated by Bruni, Pier Paolo Vergerio, and others, the notion of the humanities was based on Classical models — the tradition of a liberal arts curriculum conceived by the Greeks and elaborated by Cicero and Quintilian. Medieval scholars had been fascinated by the notion that there were seven liberal arts, no more and no less, although they did not always agree as to which they were. The humanists had their own favourites, which invariably included grammar, rhetoric, poetry, moral philosophy, and history, with a nod or two toward music and mathematics.

They also had their own ideas about methods of teaching and study. They insisted upon the mastery of Classical Latin and, where possible, Greek, which began to be studied again in the West in 1397, when the Greek scholar Manuel Chrysoloras was invited to lecture in Florence. They also insisted upon the study of Classical authors at first hand, banishing the medieval textbooks and compendiums from their schools. This greatly increased the demand for Classical texts, which was first met by copying manuscript books in the newly developed humanistic scripts and then, after the mid-15th century, by the method of printing with movable type, first developed in Germany and rapidly adopted in Italy and elsewhere. Thus, while it is true that most of the ancient authors were already known in the Middle Ages, there was an all-important difference between circulating a book in many copies to a reading public and jealously guarding a single exemplar as a prized possession in some remote monastery library.

The term humanist (Italian *umanista*, Latin *humanista*) first occurs in 15th-century documents to refer to a teacher

Italian lyric poet Petrarch. Hulton Archive/Getty Images

of the humanities. Humanists taught in a variety of ways. Some founded their own schools—as Vittorino da Feltre did in Mantua in 1423 and Guarino Veronese in Ferrara in 1429—where students could study the new curriculum at both elementary and advanced levels. Some humanists taught in universities, which, while remaining strongholds of specialization in law, medicine, and theology, had begun to make a place for the new disciplines by the late 14th century. Still others were employed in private households, as was the poet and scholar Politian (Angelo Poliziano), who was tutor to the Medici children as well as a university professor.

Formal education was only one of several ways in which the humanists shaped the minds of their age. Many were themselves fine literary artists who exemplified the eloquence they were trying to foster in their students. Renaissance Latin poetry, for example, nowadays dismissed—usually unread—as imitative and formalistic, contains much graceful and lyrical expression by such humanists as Politian, Giovanni Pontano, and Jacopo Sannazzaro. In drama, Politian, Pontano, and Pietro Bembo were important innovators, and the humanists were in their element in the composition of elegant letters, dialogues, and discourses. By the late 15th century, humanists were beginning to apply their ideas about language and literature to composition in Italian as well as in Latin, demonstrating that the "vulgar" tongue could be as supple and as elegant in poetry and prose as was Classical Latin.

CLASSICAL SCHOLARSHIP

Not every humanist was a poet, but most were Classical scholars. Classical scholarship consisted of a set of related, specialized techniques by which the cultural heritage of antiquity was made available for convenient use. Essentially, in addition to searching out and authenticating ancient authors and works, this meant editing—comparing variant manuscripts of a work, correcting faulty or doubtful passages, and commenting in notes or in separate treatises on the style, meaning, and context of an author's thought. Obviously, this demanded not only superb mastery of the languages involved and a command of Classical literature but also a knowledge of the culture that formed the ancient author's mind and influenced his writing. Consequently, the humanists created a vast scholarly literature devoted to these matters and instructive in the critical techniques of Classical philology, the study of ancient texts.

ARTS AND LETTERS

Classicism and the literary impulse went hand in hand. From Lovato Lovati and Albertino Mussato to Politian and Pontano, humanists wrote Latin poetry and drama with considerable grace and power (Politian wrote in Greek as well), while others composed epistles, essays, dialogues, treatises, and histories on Classical models. In fact, it is fair to say that the development of elegant prose was the major literary achievement of humanism and that the epistle was its typical form. Petrarch's practice of collecting, reordering, and even rewriting his letters—of treating them as works of art—was widely imitated.

For lengthier discussions, the humanist was likely to compose a formal treatise or a dialogue—a Classical form that provided the opportunity to combine literary imagination with the discussion of weighty matters. The most famous example of this type is *The Courtier*, published by Baldassare Castiglione in 1528; a graceful discussion of love, courtly manners, and the ideal education for a perfect gentleman, it had enormous influence throughout Europe. Castiglione had a humanist education, but he wrote *The Courtier* in Italian, the language Bembo chose for his dialogue on love, *Gli Asolani* (1505), and Ludovico Ariosto chose for his delightful epic, *Orlando furioso*, completed in 1516. The vernacular was coming of age as a literary medium.

According to some, a life-and-death struggle between Latin and Italian began in the 14th century, while the mortal enemies of Italian were the humanists, who impeded the natural growth of the vernacular after its brilliant beginning with Dante, Petrarch, and Boccaccio. In this view, the choice of Italian by such great 16th-century writers as Castiglione, Ariosto, and Machiavelli represents the final "triumph" of the vernacular and the restoration of contact between Renaissance culture and its native roots. The reality is somewhat less dramatic and more complicated. Most Italian writers regarded Latin as being as much a part of their culture as the vernacular, and most of them wrote in both languages. It should also be remembered that Italy was a land of powerful regional dialect traditions; until the late 13th century, Latin was the only language common to all Italians. By the end of that century, however, Tuscan was emerging as the primary vernacular, and Dante's choice of it for his *The Divine Comedy* ensured its preeminence. Of lyric poets writing in Tuscan (hereafter called Italian), the greatest was Petrarch. His *canzoni*, or songs, and sonnets in praise of Laura are revealing studies of the effect of love upon the lover; his *Italia mia* is a plea for peace that evokes the beauties of his native land; his religious songs reveal his deep spiritual feeling.

Petrarch's friend and admirer Giovanni Boccaccio is best known for his *Decameron*; but he pioneered in adapting Classical forms to Italian usage, including the hunting poem, romance, idyll, and pastoral, whereas some of his themes, most notably the story of Troilus and Cressida, were borrowed by other poets, including Geoffrey Chaucer and Torquato Tasso.

The scarcity of first-rate Italian poetry throughout most of the 15th century has caused a number of historians to regret the passing of *il buon secolo*, the great age of the language, which supposedly came to an end with the ascendancy of humanist Classicism. For every humanist who disdained the vernacular, however, there was a Leonardo Bruni to maintain its excellence or a Poggio Bracciolini to prove it in his own Italian writings. Indeed, there was an absence of first-rate Latin poets until the late 15th century, which suggests a general lack of poetic creativity in this period and not of Italian poetry alone. It may be that both Italian and Latin poets needed time to absorb and assimilate the various new tendencies of the preceding period. Tuscan was as much a new language for many as was Classical Latin, and there was a variety of literary forms to be mastered.

With Lorenzo de' Medici the period of tutelage came to an end. The Magnificent Lorenzo, virtual ruler of Florence in the late 15th century, was one of the fine poets of his time. His sonnets show Petrarch's influence, but transformed with his own genius. His poetry epitomizes the Renaissance ideal of *l'uomo universale*, the many-sided man. Love of nature, love of women, and love of life are the principal themes. The woodland settings and hunting scenes of Lorenzo's poems suggest how he found relief from a busy public life. His love songs to his mistresses and his bawdy carnival ballads show the other face of a devoted father and affectionate husband. The celebration of youth in his most famous poem was etched with the sad realization of the brevity of life. His own ended at the age of 43.

Oh, how fair is youth, and yet how fleeting! Let yourself be joyous if you feel it: Of tomorrow there is no certainty—

Florence was only one centre of the flowering of the vernacular. Ferrara saw literature and art flourish under the patronage of the ruling Este family and before the end of the 15th century counted at least one major poet, Matteo Boiardo, author of the *Orlando innamorato*, an epic of Roland. A blending of the Arthurian and Carolingian epic traditions, Boiardo's *Orlando* inspired Ludovico Ariosto to take up the same themes. The result was the finest of all Italian epics, *Orlando furioso*. The ability of the medieval epic and folk traditions to inspire the poets of such sophisticated centres as Florence and Ferrara suggests that, humanist disdain for the Dark Ages notwithstanding, Renaissance Italians did not allow Classicism to cut them off from their medieval roots.

RENAISSANCE THOUGHT

While the humanists were not primarily philosophers and belonged to no single school of formal thought, they had a great deal of influence upon philosophy. They searched out and copied the works of ancient authors, developed critical tools for establishing accurate texts from variant manuscripts, made translations from Latin and Greek, and wrote commentaries that reflected their broad learning and their new standards and points of view. Aristotle's authority remained preeminent, especially in logic and physics, but humanists were instrumental in the revival of other Greek scientists and other ancient philosophies, including stoicism, skepticism, and various forms of Platonism, as, for example, the eclectic Neoplatonist and Gnostic doctrines of the Alexandrian schools known as Hermetic philosophy. All of these were to have far-reaching effects on the subsequent development of European thought. While humanists had a variety of intellectual and scholarly aims, it is fair to say that, like the ancient Romans, they preferred moral philosophy to metaphysics. Their faith in the moral benefits of poetry and rhetoric inspired generations of scholars and educators. Their emphasis upon eloquence, worldly achievement, and fame brought them readers and patrons among merchants and princes and employment in government chancelleries and embassies.

Humanists were secularists in the sense that language, literature, politics, and history, rather than "sacred subjects," were their central interests. They defended themselves against charges from conservatives that their preference for Classical authors was ruining Christian morals and faith, arguing that a solid grounding in the Classics was the best preparation for the Christian life. This was already a perennial debate, almost as old as Christianity itself, with neither side able to prove its case. There seems to have been little atheism or dechristianization among the humanists or their pupils, although there were efforts to redefine the relationship between religious and secular culture. Petrarch struggled with the problem

Italian Renaissance ruler and poet Lorenzo de' Medici, depicted by painter Benozzo Gozzoli as traveling through the forest with an entourage. Hulton Archive/Getty Images

in his book *Secretum meum* (1342–43, revised 1353–58), in which he imagines himself chastised by St. Augustine for his pursuit of worldly fame. Even the most celebrated of Renaissance themes, the "dignity of man," best known in the *Oration* (1486) of Giovanni Pico della Mirandola, was derived in part from the Church Fathers. Created in the image and likeness of God, people were free to shape their destiny, but human destiny was defined within a Christian, Neoplatonic context of contemplative thought.

You will have the power to sink to the lower forms of life, which are brutish. You will have the power, through your own judgment, to be reborn into the higher forms, which are divine.

Perhaps because Italian politics were so intense and innovative, the tension between traditional Christian teachings and actual behaviour was more frankly acknowledged in political thought than in most other fields. The leading spokesman of the new approach to politics was Niccolò Machiavelli. Best known as the author of *The Prince* (1513), a short treatise on how to acquire power, create a state, and keep it, Machiavelli dared to argue that success in politics had its own rules. This so shocked his readers that they coined his name into synonyms for the Devil ("Old Nick") and for crafty, unscrupulous tactics (Machiavellian). No other name, except perhaps that of the Borgias, so readily evokes the image of the wicked Renaissance, and, indeed, Cesare Borgia was one of Machiavelli's chief models for *The Prince*.

Machiavelli began with the not unchristian axiom that people are immoderate in their ambitions and desires and likely to oppress each other whenever free to do so. To get them to limit their selfishness and act for the common good should be the lofty, almost holy, purpose of governments. How to establish and maintain governments that do this was the central problem of politics, made acute for Machiavelli by the twin disasters of his time, the decline of free government in the city-states and the overrunning of Italy by French, German, and Spanish armies. In *The Prince* he advocated his emergency solution: Italy needed a new leader, who would unify the people, drive out "the barbarians," and reestablish civic virtue. But in the *Discourses on the First Ten Books of Livy* (1517), a more detached and extended discussion, he analyzed the foundations and practice of republican government, still trying to explain how stubborn and defective human material was transformed into political community.

Machiavelli was influenced by humanist culture in many ways, including his reverence for Classical antiquity, his concern with politics, and his effort to evaluate the impact of fortune as against free choice in human life. The "new path" in politics that he announced in *The Prince* was an effort to provide a guide for political action based on the lessons of history and his own experience as a foreign secretary in Florence. In his passionate republicanism he showed himself to be the heir of the great humanists of a century earlier who had expounded the ideals of free citizenship and explored the uses of Classicism for the public life.

At the beginning of the 15th century, when the Visconti rulers of Milan were threatening to overrun Florence, the humanist chancellor Coluccio Salutati had rallied the Florentines by reminding them that their city was "the daughter of Rome" and the legatee of Roman justice and liberty. Salutati's pupil, Leonardo Bruni, who also served as chancellor, took up this line in his panegyrics of Florence and in his *Historiarum Florentini populi libri XII* ("Twelve Books of Histories of the Florentine People"). Even before the rise of Rome, according to Bruni, the Etruscans had founded free cities in Tuscany, so the roots of Florentine liberty went very deep. There equality was recognized in

A bust of Niccolò Machiavelli, Renaissance philosopher and statesman who espoused the then-radical idea that power trumps virtue. Hulton Archive/ Getty Images

justice and opportunity for all citizens, and the claims of individual excellence were rewarded in public offices and public honours. This close relation between freedom and achievement, argued Bruni, explained Florence's superiority in culture as well as in politics. Florence was the home of Italy's greatest poets, the pioneer in both vernacular and Latin literature, and the seat of the Greek revival and of eloquence. In short, Florence was the centre of the *studia humanitatis*.

As political rhetoric, Bruni's version of Florentine superiority was magnificent and no doubt effective. It inspired the Florentines to hold out against Milanese aggression and to reshape their identity as the seat of "the rebirth of letters" and the champions of freedom; but, as a theory of political culture, this "civic humanism," as Hans Baron has called it, represented the ideal rather than the reality of 15th-century communal history. Even in Florence, where after 1434 the Medici family held a grip on the city's republican government, opportunities for the active life began to fade. The emphasis in thought began to shift from civic humanism to Neoplatonist idealism and to the kind of utopian mysticism represented by Pico's *Oration on the Dignity of Man*.

At the end of the century, Florentines briefly put themselves into the hands of the millennialist Dominican preacher Fra Girolamo Savonarola, who envisioned the city as the "New Jerusalem" rather than as a reincarnation of ancient Rome. Still, even Savonarola borrowed from the civic tradition of the humanists for his political reforms (and for his idea of Florentine superiority) and in so doing created a bridge between the republican past and the crisis years of the early 16th century.

Machiavelli got his first job in the Florentine chancellery in 1498, the year of Savonarola's fall from power. Dismissing the friar as one of history's "unarmed prophets" who are bound to fail, Machiavelli was convinced that the precepts of Christianity had helped make the Italian states sluggish and weak. He regarded religion as an indispensable component of human life, but statecraft as a discipline based on its own rules and no more to be subordinated to Christianity than were jurisprudence or medicine. The simplest example of the difference between Christian and political morality is provided by warfare, where the use of deception, so detestable in every other kind of action, is necessary, praiseworthy, even glorious. In the *Discourses*, Machiavelli commented upon a Roman defeat:

> *This is worth noting by every citizen who is called upon to give counsel to his country, for when the very safety of the country is at stake there should be no question of justice or injustice, of mercy or cruelty, of honour or disgrace, but putting every other consideration aside, that course should be followed which will save her life and liberty.*

Machiavelli's own country was Florence. When he wrote that he loved his country more than he loved his soul, he was consciously forsaking Christian ethics for the morality of civic virtue. His friend and countryman Francesco Guicciardini shared his political morality and his concern for politics but lacked his faith that a knowledge of ancient political wisdom would redeem the liberty of Italy. Guicciardini was an upper-class Florentine who chose a career in public administration and devoted his leisure to writing history and reflecting on politics. He was steeped in the humanist traditions of Florence and was a dedicated republican, notwithstanding the fact—or perhaps because of it—that he spent his entire career in the service of the Medici and rose to high positions under them. But Guicciardini, more skeptical and aristocratic than Machiavelli, was also half a generation younger, and he was schooled in an age that was already witnessing the decline of Italian autonomy.

In 1527 Florence revolted against the Medici a second time and established a republic. As a confidant of the Medici, Guicciardini was passed over for public office and retired to his estate. One of the fruits of this enforced leisure was the so-called *Cose fiorentine* (*Florentine Affairs*), an unfinished manuscript on Florentine history. While it generally follows the classic form of humanist civic history, the fragment contains some significant departures from this tradition. No longer is the history of the city treated in isolation; Guicciardini was becoming aware that the political fortunes of Florence were interwoven with those of Italy as a whole and that the French invasion of Italy in 1494 was a turning point in Italian history. He returned to public life with the restoration of the Medici in 1530 and was involved in the events leading to the tightening of the imperial grip upon Italy, the humbling of the papacy, and the final transformation of the republic of Florence into a hereditary Medici dukedom. Frustrated in his efforts to influence the rulers of Florence, he again retired to his villa to write, but, instead of taking up the unfinished manuscript on Florentine history, he chose a subject commensurate with his changed perspective on Italian affairs. The result was his *History of Italy*. Though still in the humanist form and style, it was in substance a fulfillment of the new tendencies already evident in the earlier work—criticism of sources, great attention to detail, avoidance of moral generalizations, shrewd analysis of character and motive.

The *History of Italy* has rightly been called a tragedy by the American historian Felix Gilbert, for it demonstrates how, out of stupidity and weakness, people make mistakes that gradually narrow the range of their freedom to choose alternative courses and thus to influence events until, finally, they are trapped in the web of fortune. This view of history was already far from the world of Machiavelli, not to mention that of the civic humanists. Where Machiavelli believed that *virtù*—bold and intelligent initiative—could shape, if not totally control, *fortuna*—the play of external forces—Guicciardini was skeptical about men's ability to learn from the past and pessimistic about the individual's power to shape the course of events. All that was left, he believed, was to understand. Guicciardini wrote his histories of Florence and of Italy to show what people were like and to explain how they had reached their present circumstances. Human dignity, then, consisted not in the exercise of will to shape destiny but in the use of reason to contemplate and perhaps to tolerate fate. In taking a new, hard look at the human condition, Guicciardini represents the decline of humanist optimism.

THE NORTHERN RENAISSANCE

From Italy the humanist spirit spread north to all parts of Europe, aided by the invention of printing, which allowed literacy and the availability of Classical texts to grow explosively. As monarchies became more powerful and centralized, and as economies boomed and cities expanded, the intellectual stimulation provided by northern European humanists helped spark the Reformation—the religious revolution that became the basis for the founding of Protestantism.

POLITICAL, ECONOMIC, AND SOCIAL BACKGROUND

In 1494 King Charles VIII of France led an army southward over the Alps, seeking the Neapolitan crown and glory. Many believed that this barely literate gnome of a man, hunched over his horse, was the Second Charlemagne, whose coming had been long predicted by French and Italian prophets. Apparently, Charles himself believed this; it is recorded that, when he was chastised by Savonarola for delaying his divine mission of reform and crusade in Florence, the king burst into tears and soon went on his way. He found the Kingdom of Naples easy to take and impossible to hold. Frightened by local uprisings, by a new Italian coalition, and by the massing of Spanish troops in Sicily, he left Naples in the spring of 1495, bound not for the Holy Land, as the prophecies had predicted, but for home, never to return to Italy. In 1498 Savonarola was tortured, hanged, and burned as a false prophet for predicting that Charles would complete his mission. Conceived amid dreams of chivalric glory and crusade, the Italian expedition of Charles VIII was the venture of a medieval king—romantic, poorly planned, and totally irrelevant to the real needs of his subjects.

The French invasion of Italy marked the beginning of a new phase of European politics, during which the Valois kings of France and the Habsburgs of Germany fought each other, with the Italian states as their reluctant pawns. For the next 60 years the dream of Italian conquest was pursued by every French king, none of them having learned anything from Charles VIII's misadventure except that the road southward was open and paved with easy victories. For even longer Italy would be the keystone of the arch that the Habsburgs tried to erect across Europe from the Danube to the Strait of Gibraltar in order to link the Spanish and German inheritance of the emperor Charles V. In destroying the autonomy of Italian politics, the invasions also ended the Italian state system, which was absorbed into the larger European system that now took shape. Its members adopted the balance-of-power diplomacy first evolved by the Italians as well as the Italian practice of using resident ambassadors who combined diplomacy with the gathering of intelligence by fair means or foul. In the art of war, also, the Italians were innovators in the use of mercenary troops, cannonry, bastioned fortresses, and field fortification. French artillery was already the best in Europe by 1494, whereas the Spaniards developed the tercio, an infantry unit that combined the most effective field fortifications and weaponry of the Italians and Swiss.

Thus, old and new ways were fused in the bloody crucible of the Italian Wars. Rulers who lived by medieval codes of chivalry adopted Renaissance techniques of diplomacy and warfare to satisfy their lust for glory and dynastic power. Even the lure of Italy was an old obsession, but the size and vigour of the 16th-century expeditions were new. Rulers were now able to command vast quantities of men and resources because they were becoming masters of their own domains. The nature and degree of this mastery varied according to local circumstances, but throughout Europe the New Monarchs, as they are called, were reasserting kingship as the dominant form of political leadership after a long period of floundering and uncertainty.

By the end of the 15th century, the Valois kings of France had expelled the English from all their soil except the port of Calais, concluding the Hundred Years' War (1453), had incorporated the fertile lands of the duchy of Burgundy to the east and of Brittany to the north, and had extended the French kingdom from the Atlantic and the English Channel to the Pyrenees and the Rhine. To rule this vast territory, they created a professional machinery of state, converting wartime taxing privileges into permanent prerogative, freeing their royal council from supervision by the Estates-General, appointing a host of officials who crisscrossed the kingdom in the service of the crown, and establishing their right to appoint and tax the French clergy. They did not achieve anything like complete centralization, but in 1576 Jean Bodin was able to write, in his *Six Books of the Commonweal*, that the king of France had absolute sovereignty because he alone in the kingdom had the power to give law unto all of his subjects in general and to every one of them in particular.

Bodin might also have made his case by citing the example of another impressive autocrat of his time, Philip II of Spain. Though descended from warrior kings, Philip spent his days at his writing desk poring over dispatches from his governors in the Low Countries, Sicily, Naples, Milan, Peru, Mexico, and the Philippines and drafting his orders to them in letters signed "I the King." The founding of this mighty empire went back more than a century to 1469, when Ferdinand II of Aragon and Isabella of Castile brought two great Hispanic kingdoms together under a single dynasty. Castile, an arid land of sheepherders, great landowning churchmen, and crusading knights, and Aragon, with its Catalan miners and its strong ties to Mediterranean Europe, made uneasy partners, but a series of rapid and energetic actions forced the process of national consolidation and catapulted the new nation into a position of world prominence for which it was poorly prepared.

Within the last decade of the 15th century, the Spaniards took the kingdom of Navarre in the north; stormed the last Muslim stronghold in Spain, the kingdom of Granada; and launched a campaign of religious unification by pressing tens of thousands of Muslims and Jews to choose between baptism and expulsion, at the same time establishing a new Inquisition under royal control. They also sent Columbus on voyages of discovery to the Western Hemisphere, thereby opening a new frontier just as the domestic frontier of reconquest was closing. Finally, the crown linked its destinies with the Habsburgs by a double marriage, thus projecting Spain into the heart of European politics.

In the following decades, Castilian hidalgos (lower nobles), whose fathers had crusaded against the Moors in Spain, streamed across the Atlantic to make their fortunes out of the land and sweat of the American Indians, while others marched in the armies and sailed in the ships of their king, Charles I, who, as Charles V, was elected Holy Roman emperor in 1519 at the age of 19. In this youth, the vast dual inheritance of the Spanish and Habsburg empires came together. The grandson of Ferdinand and Isabella on his mother's side and of the emperor Maximilian I on his father's, Charles was duke of Burgundy, head of five Austrian dukedoms (which he ceded to his brother), king of Naples, Sicily, and Sardinia, and claimant to the duchy of Milan as well as king of Aragon and Castile and German king and emperor. To administer this enormous legacy, he presided over an ever-increasing bureaucracy of viceroys, governors, judges, military captains, and an army of clerks. The New World lands were governed by a separate Council of the Indies after 1524, which, like Charles' other royal councils, combined judicial, legislative, military, and fiscal functions.

The yield in American treasure was enormous, especially after the opening of the silver mines of Mexico and what is now Bolivia halfway through the 16th century. The crown skimmed off a lion's share—usually a fifth—which it paid out immediately to its creditors because everything Charles could raise by taxing or borrowing was sucked up by his wars against the French in Italy and Burgundy, the Protestant princes in Germany, the Turks on the Austrian border, and the Barbary pirates in the Mediterranean. By 1555 both Charles and his credit were exhausted, and he began to relinquish his titles—Spain and the Netherlands to his son Philip, Germany and the imperial title to his brother Ferdinand I. American silver did little for Spain except to pay the wages of soldiers and sailors; the goods and services that kept the Spanish armies in the field and the ships afloat were largely supplied by foreigners, who reaped the profits. Yet, for the rest of the century, Spain continued to dazzle the world, and few could see the chinks in the armour; this was an age of kings, in which bold deeds, not balance sheets, made history.

The growth of centralized monarchy claiming absolute sovereignty over its subjects may be observed in other places, from the England of Henry VIII on the extreme west of Europe to the Muscovite tsardom of Ivan III the Great on its eastern edge, for the New Monarchy was one aspect of a more general phenomenon—a great recovery that surged through Europe in the 15th century. No single cause can be adduced to explain it. Some historians believe it was simply the upturn in the natural cycle of growth: the great medieval population boom had overextended Europe's productive capacities; the depression of the 14th and early 15th centuries had corrected this condition through famines and epidemics, leading to depopulation; now the cycle of growth was beginning again.

Once more, growing numbers of people, burgeoning cities, and ambitious governments were demanding food, goods, and services—a demand that was met by both old and new methods of production. In agriculture, the shift toward commercial crops such as wool and grains, the investment of capital, and the emancipation of servile labour completed the transformation of the manorial system already in decline. (In eastern Europe, however, the formerly free peasantry was now forced into serfdom by an alliance between the monarchy and the landed gentry, as huge agrarian estates were formed to raise grain for an expanding Western market.) Manufacturing boomed, especially of those goods used in the outfitting of armies

*Emperor Charles V. King of Spain from 1516, Charles was also named Holy
Roman emperor in 1519, making him the most powerful monarch in Europe.*
Hulton Archive/Getty Images

and fleets—cloth, armour, weapons, and ships. New mining and metalworking technology made possible the profitable exploitation of the rich iron, copper, gold, and silver deposits of central Germany, Hungary, and Austria, affording the opportunity for large-scale investment of capital.

One index of Europe's recovery is the spectacular growth of certain cities. Antwerp, for example, more than doubled its population in the second half of the 15th century and doubled it again by 1560. Under Habsburg patronage, Antwerp became the chief European entrepôt for English cloth, the hub of an international banking network, and the principal Western market for German copper and silver, Portuguese spices, and Italian alum. By 1500 the Antwerp Bourse was the central money market for much of Europe. Other cities profited from their special circumstances, too: Lisbon as the home port for the Portuguese maritime empire; Sevilla (Seville), the Spaniards' gateway to the New World; London, the capital of the Tudors and gathering point for England's cloth-making and banking activity; Lyon, favoured by the French kings as a market centre and capital of the silk industry; and Augsburg, the principal north-south trade route in Germany and the home city of the Fugger merchant-bankers.

NORTHERN HUMANISM

Cities were also markets for culture. The resumption of urban growth in the second half of the 15th century coincided with the diffusion of Renaissance ideas and educational values. Humanism offered linguistic and rhetorical skills that were becoming indispensable for nobles and commoners seeking careers in diplomacy and government administration, while the Renaissance ideal of the perfect gentleman was a cultural style that had great appeal in this age of growing courtly refinement. At first many who wanted a humanist education went to Italy, and many foreign names appear on the rosters of the Italian universities. By the end of the century, however, such northern cities as London, Paris, Antwerp, and Augsburg were becoming centres of humanist activity rivaling Italy's. The development of printing, by making books cheaper and more plentiful, also quickened the diffusion of humanism.

A textbook convention, heavily armoured against truth by constant reiteration, states that northern humanism—i.e., humanism outside Italy—was essentially Christian in spirit and purpose, in contrast to the essentially secular nature of Italian humanism. In fact, however, the program of Christian humanism had been laid out by Italian humanists of the stamp of Lorenzo Valla, one of the founders of Classical philology, who showed how the critical methods used to study the Classics ought to be applied to problems of biblical exegesis and translation as well as church history. That this program only began to be carried out in the 16th century, particularly in the countries of northern Europe (and Spain), is a matter of chronology rather than of geography. In the 15th century, the necessary skills, particularly the knowledge of Greek, were possessed by a few scholars. A century later, Greek was a regular part of the humanist curriculum, and Hebrew was becoming much better known, particularly after Johannes Reuchlin published his Hebrew grammar in 1506. Here, too, printing was a crucial factor, for it made available a host of lexicographical and grammatical handbooks and allowed the establishment of normative biblical texts and the comparison of different versions of the Bible.

Christian humanism was more than a program of scholarship, however; it was fundamentally a conception of the Christian life that was grounded in the rhetorical, historical, and ethical orientation of humanism itself. That it came to the fore in the early 16th century was the result of a variety of factors, including the spiritual stresses of rapid social change and the inability of the ecclesiastical establishment to cope with the religious needs of an increasingly literate and self-confident laity. By restoring the gospel to the centre of Christian piety, the humanists believed they were better serving the needs of ordinary people. They attacked scholastic theology as an arid intellectualization of simple faith, and they deplored the tendency of religion to become a ritual practiced vicariously through a priest. They also despised the whole late-medieval apparatus of relic mongering, hagiology, indulgences, and image worship, and they ridiculed it in their writings, sometimes with devastating effect. According to the Christian humanists, the fundamental law of Christianity was the law of love as revealed by Jesus Christ in the Gospel. Love, peace, and simplicity should be the aims of the good Christian, and the life of Christ his perfect model. The chief spokesman for this point of view was Desiderius Erasmus, the most influential humanist of his day. Erasmus and his colleagues were uninterested in dogmatic differences and were early champions of religious toleration. In this they were not in tune with the changing times, for the outbreak of the Reformation polarized European society along confessional lines, with the paradoxical result that the Christian humanists, who had done so much to lay the groundwork for religious reform, ended by being suspect on both sides—by the Roman Catholics as subversives who (as it was said of Erasmus) had "laid the egg that Luther hatched" and by the Protestants as hypocrites who had abandoned the cause of reformation out of cowardice or ambition. Toleration belonged to the future, after the killing in the name of Christ sickened and passions had cooled.

CHRISTIAN MYSTICS

The quickening of the religious impulse that gave rise
to Christian humanism was also manifested in a variety
of forms of religious devotion among the laity, including
mysticism. In the 14th century a wave of mystical ardour
seemed to course down the valley of the Rhine, envel-
oping men and women in the rapture of intense, direct
experience of the divine Spirit. It centred in the houses
of the Dominican order, where friars and nuns practiced
the mystical way of their great teacher, Meister Eckhart.
This wave of Rhenish mysticism radiated beyond con-
vent walls to the marketplaces and hearths of the laity.
Eckhart had the gift of making his abstruse doctrines
understandable to a wider public than was usual for mystics; moreover, he was fortunate in having some disciples
of a genius almost equal to his own—the great preacher
of practical piety, Johann Tauler, and Heinrich Suso,
whose devotional books, such as *The Little Book of Truth*
and *The Little Book of Eternal Wisdom*, reached eager lay
readers hungry for spiritual consolation and religious
excitement. Some found it by joining the Dominicans;
others, remaining in the everyday world, joined with
like-spirited brothers and sisters in groups known collectively as the Friends of God, where they practiced
methodical contemplation, or, as it was widely known,
mental prayer. Probably few reached, or even hoped to
reach, the ecstasy of mystical union, which was limited
to those with the appropriate psychological or spiritual
gifts. Out of these circles came the anonymous *German
Theology*, from which, Luther was to say, he had learned
more about man and God than from any book except the
Bible and the writings of St. Augustine.

In the Netherlands the mystical impulse awakened
chiefly under the stimulus of another great teacher,

Gerhard Groote. Not a monk nor even a priest, Groote gave the mystical movement a different direction by teaching that true spiritual communion must be combined with moral action, for this was the whole lesson of the Gospel. At his death a group of followers formed the Brethren of the Common Life. These were laymen and laywomen, married and single, earning their livings in the world but united by a simple rule that required them to pool their earnings and devote themselves to spiritual works, teaching, and charity. Houses of Brothers and Sisters of the Common Life spread through the cities and towns of the Netherlands and Germany, and a monastic counterpart was founded in the order of Canons Regular of St. Augustine, known as the Windesheim Congregation, which in the second half of the 15th century numbered some 82 priories. The Brethren were particularly successful as schoolmasters, combining some of the new linguistic methods of the humanists with a strong emphasis upon Bible study. Among the generations of children who absorbed the new piety (*devotio moderna*) in their schools were Erasmus and, briefly, Luther. In the ambience of the *devotio moderna* appeared one of the most influential books of piety ever written, *The Imitation of Christ*, attributed to Thomas à Kempis, a monk of the Windesheim Congregation.

One man whose life was changed by *The Imitation* was the 16th-century Spaniard Ignatius of Loyola. After reading it, Loyola founded the Society of Jesus and wrote his own book of methodical prayer, *Spiritual Exercises*. Thus, Spanish piety was in some ways connected with that of the Netherlands; but the extraordinary outburst of mystical and contemplative activity in 16th-century Spain was mainly an expression of the intense religious exaltation of the Spanish people themselves as they confronted the tasks of reform, Counter-Reformation, and world leadership. Spanish mysticism belies the usual picture of the mystic as a withdrawn contemplative, with his or her head in the clouds. Not only Loyola but also St. Teresa of Avila and her disciple, St. John of the Cross, were tough, activist Reformers who regarded their mystical experiences as means of fortifying themselves for their practical tasks. They were also prolific writers who could communicate their experiences and analyze them for the benefit of others. This is especially true of St. John of the Cross, whose mystical poetry is one of the glories of Spanish literature.

THE GROWTH OF VERNACULAR LITERATURE

In literature, medieval forms continued to dominate the artistic imagination throughout the 15th century. Besides the vast devotional literature of the period—the *ars moriendi*, or books on the art of dying well, the saints' lives, and manuals of methodical prayer and spiritual consolation—the most popular reading of noble and burgher alike was a 13th-century love allegory, the *Roman de la rose*. Despite a promising start in the late Middle Ages, literary creativity suffered from the domination of Latin as the language of "serious" expression, with the result that, if the vernacular attracted writers, they tended to overload it with Latinisms and artificially applied rhetorical forms. This was the case with the so-called *grands rhetoriqueurs* of Burgundy and France. One exception is 14th-century England, where a national literature made a brilliant showing in the works of William Langland, John Gower, and, above all, Geoffrey Chaucer. The troubled 15th century, however, produced only feeble imitations. Another exception is the vigorous tradition of chronicle writing in French, distinguished by such eminently readable works as the chronicle of Jean Froissart and the memoirs of Philippe de Commynes. In France, too, about the middle of the 15th century there lived the vagabond François Villon, a great poet about whom next to nothing is known. In Germany *The Ship of Fools*, by Sebastian Brant, was a lone masterpiece.

The 16th century saw a true renaissance of national literatures. In Protestant countries, the Reformation had an enormous impact upon the quantity and quality of literary output. If Luther's rebellion destroyed the chances of unifying the nation politically—because religious division exacerbated political division and made Lutherans intolerant of the Catholic Habsburgs—his translation of the Bible into German created a national language. Biblical translations, vernacular liturgies, hymns, and sacred drama had analogous effects elsewhere. For Roman Catholics, especially in Spain, the Reformation was a time of deep religious emotion expressed in art and literature. On all sides of the religious controversy, chroniclers and historians writing in the vernacular were recording their versions for posterity.

While the Reformation was providing a subject matter, the Italian Renaissance was providing literary methods and models. The Petrarchan sonnet inspired French, English, and Spanish poets, while the Renaissance neoclassical drama finally began to end the reign of the medieval mystery play. Ultimately, of course, the works of real genius were the result of a crossing of native traditions and new forms. The Frenchman François Rabelais assimilated all the themes of his day—and mocked them all—in his story of the giants Gargantua and Pantagruel. The Spaniard Miguel de Cervantes, in *Don Quixote*, drew a composite portrait of his countrymen, which caught their exact mixture of idealism and realism. In England, Christopher Marlowe and William Shakespeare used Renaissance drama to probe the deeper levels of their countrymen's character and experiences.

RENAISSANCE SCIENCE AND TECHNOLOGY

According to medieval scientists, matter was composed of four elements—earth, air, fire, and water—whose combinations and permutations made up the world of visible objects. The cosmos was a series of concentric spheres in motion, the farther ones carrying the stars around in their daily courses. At the centre was the globe of Earth, heavy and static. Motion was either perfectly circular, as in the heavens, or irregular and naturally downward, as on Earth. The Earth had three landmasses—Europe, Asia, and Africa—and was unknown and uninhabitable in its southern zones. Human beings, the object of all creation, were composed of four humours—black and yellow bile, blood, and phlegm—and the body's health was determined by the relative proportions of each. The cosmos was alive with a universal consciousness with which people could interact in various ways, and the heavenly bodies were generally believed to influence human character and events, although theologians worried about free will.

These views were an amalgam of Classical and Christian thought and, from what can be inferred from written sources, shaped the way educated people experienced and interpreted phenomena. What people who did not read or write books understood about nature is more difficult to tell, except that belief in magic, good and evil spirits, witchcraft, and forecasting the future was universal. The church might prefer that Christians seek their well-being through faith, the sacraments, and the intercession of Mary and the saints, but distinctions between acceptable and unacceptable belief in hidden powers were difficult to make or to maintain. Most clergy shared the common beliefs in occult forces and lent their authority to them. The collaboration of formal doctrine and popular belief had some of its most terrible consequences during the Renaissance, such as pogroms against Jews and witch-hunts, in which the church provided the doctrines of Satanic conspiracy and the inquisitorial agents and popular prejudice supplied the victims, predominantly women and marginal people.

Among the formally educated, if not among the general population, traditional science was transformed by the new heliocentric, mechanistic, and mathematical conceptions of Copernicus, Harvey, Kepler, Galileo, and Newton. Historians of science are increasingly reluctant to describe these changes as a revolution, since this implies too sudden and complete an overthrow of the earlier model. Aristotle's authority gave way very slowly, and only the first of the great scientists mentioned above did his work in the period under consideration. Still, the Renaissance made some important contributions toward the process of paradigm shift, as the 20th-century historian of science Thomas Kuhn called major innovations in science. Humanist scholarship provided both originals and translations of ancient Greek scientific works—which enormously increased the fund of knowledge in physics, astronomy, medicine, botany, and other disciplines—and presented as well alternative theories to those of Ptolemy and Aristotle. Thus, the revival of ancient science brought heliocentric astronomy to the fore again after almost two millennia. Renaissance philosophers, most notably Jacopo Zabarella, analyzed and formulated the rules of the deductive and inductive methods by which scientists worked, while certain ancient philosophies enriched the ways in which scientists conceived of phenomena. Pythagoreanism, for example, conveyed a vision of a harmonious geometric universe that helped form the mind of Copernicus.

In mathematics the Renaissance made its greatest contribution to the rise of modern science. Humanists included arithmetic and geometry in the liberal arts curriculum; artists furthered the geometrization of space in their work on perspective; Leonardo da Vinci perceived, however faintly, that the world was ruled by "number." The interest in algebra in the Renaissance universities, according to the 20th-century historian of science George Sarton, "was creating a kind of fever." It produced some mathematical theorists of the first rank, including Niccolò Tartaglia and Girolamo Cardano. If they had done nothing else, Renaissance scholars would have made a great contribution to mathematics by translating and publishing, in 1544, some previously unknown works of Archimedes, perhaps the most important of the ancients in this field.

If the Renaissance role in the rise of modern science was more that of midwife than of parent, in the realm of technology the proper image is the Renaissance magus, manipulator of the hidden forces of nature. Working with medieval perceptions of natural processes, engineers and technicians of the 15th and 16th centuries achieved remarkable results and pushed the traditional cosmology to the limit of its explanatory powers. This may have had more to do with changing social needs than with changes in scientific theory. Warfare was one catalyst of practical change that stimulated new theoretical questions. With the spread of the use of artillery, for example, questions about the motion of bodies in space became more insistent, and mathematical calculation more critical. The manufacture of guns also stimulated metallurgy and fortification; town planning and reforms in the standards of measurement were related to problems of geometry. The Renaissance preoccupation with alchemy, the parent of chemistry, was certainly stimulated by the shortage of precious metals, made more acute by the expansion of government and expenditures on war.

The most important technological advance of all, because it underlay progress in so many other fields, strictly speaking, had little to do with nature. This was the development of printing, with movable metal type, about the mid-15th century in Germany. Johannes Gutenberg is usually called its inventor, but in fact many people and many steps were involved. Block printing on wood came to the West from China between 1250 and 1350, papermaking came from China by way of the Arabs to 12th-century Spain, whereas the Flemish technique of oil painting was the origin of the new printers' ink. Three men of Mainz—Gutenberg and his contemporaries Johann Fust and Peter Schöffer—seem to have taken the final steps, casting metal type and locking it into a wooden press. The invention spread like the wind, reaching Italy by 1467, Hungary and Poland in the 1470s, and Scandinavia by 1483. By 1500 the presses of Europe had produced some six million books. Without the printing press it is impossible to conceive that the Reformation would have ever been more than a monkish quarrel or that the rise of a new science, which was a cooperative effort of an international community, would have occurred at all. In short, the development of printing amounted to a communications revolution of the order of the invention of writing; and, like that prehistoric discovery, it transformed the conditions of life. The communications revolution immeasurably enhanced human opportunities for enlightenment and pleasure on one hand and created previously undreamed-of possibilities for manipulation and control on the other. The consideration of such contradictory effects may guard us against a ready acceptance of triumphalist conceptions of the Renaissance or of historical change in general.

CONCLUSION

The first several thousand years of European history, as well as the preceding millennia of prehistory, were characterized by numerous technological, social, political, economic, and cultural innovations. Following the appearance of modern humans in Europe about 35,000 BC, the prehistoric peoples of the Paleolithic Period, or Old Stone Age, gradually improved the stone tools that aided them in their hunting and gathering lifestyle. At the end of the Paleolithic, humans began to cultivate crops; the widespread adoption of agriculture marked the start of the Neolithic Period, or New Stone Age. The Stone Ages were succeeded by the Metal Ages of the 3rd to 1st millennia BC, when European peoples began producing and working copper, then bronze, and then iron. By the end of the Metal Ages, a wide variety of languages were spoken throughout Europe, the majority of them belonging to the Indo-European language group. In southeastern Europe, the speakers of Greek dialects became the first of these Indo-European groups to adopt a writing system.

Writing—the use of which marks the end of prehistory and the beginning of recorded history—was just one of the many accomplishments of the advanced civilizations that arose in the Aegean region in the 2nd millennium BC. The ancient Greek period was a time of unparalleled political, artistic, and intellectual achievements that had a lasting influence on European civilization, beginning with that of the ancient Romans. Rome grew from a small town in central Italy in the 1st millennium BC into a vast empire that, at its greatest extent in the 2nd century AD, embraced southern Britain and all of continental Europe west of the Rhine and south of the Danube. Consequently, the Romans imprinted their culture—one aspect of which, in the late stages of the empire, was Christianity—on much

Engraving depicting Johannes Gutenberg and two compatriots checking a proof created by Gutenberg's printing press, one of the most important technical advances of the Renaissance. Kean Collection/Hulton Archive/ Getty Images

of the Continent. After a series of internal and external crises, the western part of the empire fell to invading Germanic peoples in the 5th century AD, while the eastern portion continued on as the Greek-influenced Byzantine Empire.

The eclipse of the Western Roman Empire, which had provided cohesion for much of the Continent, had an enormous impact on the political structure and social climate of western Europe. In the early Middle Ages, no large kingdom or other political structure—apart from the Carolingian court established by Charlemagne— arose in Europe to provide stability. In this environment, often described as feudal, political authority was diffused among various local lords. The only force capable of providing social unity was Christianity. Thus arose the idea of Europe as a large church-state, called Christendom. Yet the old Roman division between western and eastern Europe persisted within the Christian church, which formally split in 1054. Thereafter, Roman Catholicism dominated in the West, while Eastern Orthodoxy presided over the East. Meanwhile, as the Middle Ages progressed, towns began to flourish, merchant classes began to develop, and agricultural developments contributed to the expansion of the population. These and other factors led to the breakup of the feudal structures that had characterized much of the Middle Ages.

The crumbling of feudalism, the strengthening of city-states in Italy, and the emergence of powerful national monarchies, as well as the rise of secular education, culminated in the philosophical and cultural revival known as the Renaissance. Humanism, as the intellectual movement behind the Renaissance was known, spread from Italy to northern and western Europe, where, aided by the invention of the printing press, it contributed to the outbreak of the Protestant Reformation. By the end of the 16th century, the battle between Protestantism and the Roman Catholic Church, which had launched its own Counter-Reformation, commanded much of Europe's attention. The early modern period of European history had begun.

GLOSSARY

acropolis The fortified height of an ancient Greek city, containing municipal and religious buildings.

adoptionism The Christian heresy that holds that Jesus of Nazareth is the Son of God by adoption.

amphora One of the principal vessel shapes in Greek pottery, a two-handled pot with a narrow neck.

anchorite A person who lives as a recluse for religious purposes.

Arian Pertaining to the doctrine of Arius, which holds that Jesus and God are of different substances.

barrow An ancient burial place covered with a large mound of earth or stones.

cairn A pile of stones used as a boundary marker, a memorial, or a burial site.

cenobitic monasticism Form of monasticism characterized by strict discipline, regular worship, and manual work.

chancery An office of public records or archives.

conciliar Pertaining to or issued by a council.

dialectic A form of logical argumentation.

exegesis Critical analysis of a text, especially a religious text.

faience Glazed pottery, especially of a fine variety with highly coloured designs.

heterodox Incompatible with or different from the standards of an accepted religion or belief system.

hoard A cache of hidden objects.

hominin A term used most often to refer to extinct members of the human lineage.

inhumation Burial in graves.

magisterium The authority of the Roman Catholic
Church to impose its doctrine upon the learner under
a religious and moral obligation.

market economy The production and distribution of
goods and services through a free market.

mendicant A member of any of several Roman Catholic
religious orders who assumes a vow of poverty and
supports himself or herself by work and charitable
contributions.

nicolaitism The practice of allowing members of the
clergy to marry.

obscurantism The practice of concealing information
from the public.

oppidum A fortified town.

palace economy The distribution of wealth from a central authority to the general public; also referred to as
a redistributive economy.

palisade A structure erected for defense, consisting of
several stakes placed in the ground in a fence-like
formation.

pogrom The organized persecution of a specific group.

simony Buying or selling of something spiritual or
closely connected with the spiritual, particularly
church offices. More widely, it is any contract of this
kind forbidden by divine or ecclesiastical law.

theogony The account of the gods' origins.

tonsure In various religions, a ceremony of initiation
in which hair is clipped from the head as part of the
ritual marking one's entrance into a new stage of religious development or activity.

wattle A building cover composed of poles through
which reeds or branches have been woven

BIBLIOGRAPHY

A comprehensive introduction to European prehistory is offered in Timothy Champion et al., *Prehistoric Europe* (1984). Specific periods are covered in Clive Gamble, *The Palaeolithic Settlement of Europe* (1986); Clive Bonsall (ed.), *The Mesolithic in Europe* (1989); and Alasdair Whittle, *Neolithic Europe: A Survey* (1985). A good account of the Indo-Europeans is J.P. Mallory, *In Search of the Indo-Europeans: Language, Archaeology, and Myth* (1989). Marie Louise Stig Sørensen and Roger Thomas (eds.), *The Bronze Age–Iron Age Transition in Europe: Aspects of Continuity and Change in European Societies, c. 1200 to 500 BC*, 2 vol. (1989), is a collection of scholarly articles on the Metal Ages.

Barry Cunliffe, *Greeks, Romans, and Barbarians: Spheres of Interaction* (1988), explores the influence of Classical civilization and commerce on the cultures of central and western Europe. Detailed treatments of ancient Greek civilization include N.G.L. Hammond, *A History of Greece to 322 BC*, 3rd ed. (1986); and J.B. Bury and Russell Meiggs, *A History of Greece to the Death of Alexander the Great*, 4th ed. (1975). H.H. Scullard, *A History of the Roman World: 753–146 BC*, 4th ed. (1980), is a standard comprehensive survey. Another relevant history is William V. Harris, *War and Imperialism in Republican Rome, 327–70 BC* (1979, reprinted 1985), on Roman expansion. Michael Grant and Rachel Kitzinger (eds.), *Civilization of the Ancient Mediterranean: Greece and Rome*, 3 vol. (1988), is a comprehensive collection of essays on cultural, economic, and social life in the Classical world. A discussion of late antiquity is G.W. Bowersock, Peter Brown, and Oleg Grabar (eds.), *Late Antiquity: A Guide to the Postclassical World* (1999).

Useful reference works on the Middle Ages are *The New Cambridge Medieval History*, 7 vol. (1995–2005); and *Encyclopedia of the Middle Ages*, 2 vol. (2000). Two important volumes that represent scholarly perspectives of the late 20th and early 21st century are Peter Linehan and Janet L. Nelson, *The Medieval World* (2001); and Lester K. Little and Barbara Rosenwein (eds.), *Debating the Middle Ages: Issues and Readings* (1998). Historical surveys of the medieval period include Rosamond McKitterick (ed.), *The Early Middle Ages: Europe, 400–1000* (2001); R.I. Moore, *The First European Revolution, c. 970–1215* (2000); and David Nicholas, *The Transformation of Europe 1300–1600* (1999).

The Renaissance is examined in Thomas A. Brady, Heiko A. Oberman, and James D. Tracy (eds.), *Handbook of European History, 1400–1600: Late Middle Ages, Renaissance, and Reformation*, 2 vol. (1994–95); and Lauro Martines, *Power and Imagination: City States in Renaissance Italy* (1988). Donald Kelley, *Renaissance Humanism* (1991), discusses humanist thought and influence. Elizabeth L. Eisenstein, *The Printing Revolution in Early Modern Europe* (1983), makes a strong case for the revolutionary impact of Renaissance print technology upon culture.

INDEX

A

Abelard, Peter, 134
Achaean League, 73–74
adoptionism, 117, 119
Adrian I, 119
Aeolians, 69
Aethelberht of Kent, 110
Aëtius, 85
age, burial practices and, 29,
    45–46
agriculture
    Indo-European, 22–23
    Iron Age, 35–36
    Mesolithic Period, 8, 12
    Middle Ages, 123–126
    Neolithic Period, 13–20
    Paleolithic Period, 5
Alaric II, 86
Alcuin, 117
Alemanni, 82, 83, 85
Alexander III (pope), 132
Alexander the Great, 92
Alfred the Great, 117
alliances, 83–85
alloys, use of, 31, 33
Ambrones, 81
Ambrose of Milan, 104
Anastasius, 115
Angles, 85
Annales Ecclesiastici (Casear
    Baronius), 94
Apostolic Camera, 140
Aquinas, Thomas, 89, 137

Arianism, 86–87, 106, 110
Ariosto, Ludovico, 178, 180
Ariovistus, 81
aristocracy
    burial practices and, 45–46
    marriage among, 157, 191–192
    Middle Ages, 108–109,
        124–126, 152–158
    Renaissance, 188–195
Aristotelianism, 136–137
Aristotle, 156, 203
armour, 33
Arnold of Brescia, 140
Arnulfing-Pippinid family, 115

ars moriendi, 200
Athanasius of Alexandria, 105
athletics, Greek, 70
Attila the Hun, 85
Augustine of Canterbury, 110
Augustine of Hippo, 92–93, 109,
    182, 198, 199
Augustus, 81, 101
Avars, 88
Avignon papacy, 140

B

Barbarians, 80–88, 103
Baron, Hans, 185
Baronius, Casear, 94
Battle-Ax people, 80
Bavarians, 86
Bede, 100–101, 111, 112, 117

Beguines, 144, 146
Belisarius, 87
Bell Beaker culture, 21, 29, 45
Bembo, Pietro, 176, 177–178
Benedict of Nursia, 104–105
Biscop, Benedict, 111
bishops of Rome, 104, 111–114
Black Death, 159
Boccaccio, Giovanni, 178
Bodin, Jean, 191
Boiardo, Matteo, 180
Bonaventure, 137
Boniface of Mainz, 111, 117
Brant, Sebastian, 201
Brethren of the Common Life, 199
Bronze Age, 20, 24–26, 29–35,
    38–45, 54
  building/settlement during,
    33–35
  burial practices during, 29, 45–46
  culture during, 25–27, 29–35,
    42, 55–62
  gender during, 29
  Germanic people during, 80
  military during, 33–35
  religion during, 55–62
  stages A-D, 26
  technology during, 30, 33
  trade during, 25, 26, 30
Bruni, Leonardo, 173–174, 179,
    183, 185
building/settlement
  Bronze Age, 33–35
  Copper Age, 28
  Iron Age, 36
  Mesolithic Period, 12
  Middle Ages, 127–128
  Neolithic Period, 15, 16, 20–21
  Paleolithic Period, 5

Burckhardt, Jacob, 97, 163, 167, 169
Burgundians, 86
burial practices
  age and, 29, 45–46
  aristocracy and, 45–46
  Bronze Age, 29, 45–46
  Copper Age, 28
  gender and, 29, 45–46
  Iron Age, 52–54
  Mesolithic Period, 12
  Metal Ages, 24, 25, 40–46
  Neolithic Period, 15, 16, 21–22
  Paleolithic Period, 4, 6
Byzantine Empire, 73–74, 151

C

Caesar, Julius, 81
Caesarius of Arles, 109
calendar, 100–101
Cambridge Medieval History, 98
Cange, Charles du Fresne,
    Seigneur du, 95
Caracalla, 77
Cardano, Girolamo, 204
Carlowitz, Treaty of, 151
Carolingian dynasty, 89,
    115–124
Carolingian Renaissance, 171
Cassian, John, 105
Castiglione, Baldassare, 177–178
Celestine III, 140
celibacy, 130
Celtic art style, 27, 31
Celtic Christianity, 110–111
Centuriae Magdeburgensis
    (Matthias Flacius Illyricus), 94
Cervantes, Miguel de, 201
Chalcolithic Period, 27

Charlemagne, 88, 89, 92, 115–120, 121
Charles IV (emperor), 133
Charles V (emperor), 189, 192–193
Charles VIII of France, 188–189
Chaucer, Geoffrey, 178, 200
Christian humanism, 196–198
Christianity
  devotional life, 143–147
  ecclesiastical discipline, 147–149
  ecclesiastical organization, 137–143
  the Great Commission and, 109–111
  impact of on historical study, 92–95
  Islam and, 149–151
  Judaism and, 149–151
  Middle Ages, 101–151
  organization of imperial, 103–108
  papacy and, 111–114
  Reformation, 129–152, 198
  Renaissance, 198–200
  Romans and, 78–80, 101–114
  spread of, 86–87
  types of, 105–106
Christology, 106
Chrysolaras, Manuel, 174
Cicero, 156, 173, 174
Cimbri, 81
Cistercians, 144
citizenry, under Romans, 77
City of God (Augustine of Hippo), 92
Civilization of the Renaissance in Italy, The (Jacob Burckhardt), 97, 163

classical scholarship, during Renaissance, 176–177
Clement II, 130
clergy, during Middle Ages, 104–105, 111–114, 119–120, 129–152
climate
  Mesolithic Period, 8, 10–12
  Neolithic Period, 20
  Paleolithic Period, 4, 5, 8
Clotilda, 110
Clovis, 86, 110
Clovis I, 115
College of Cardinals, 139
coloni, 102
Columba (monk), 110
Columban (monk), 110
Concordia discordantium canonum, 134
condottiere, 167
Confessions (Augustine of Hippo), 109
Conrad I, 120
consistory, 140
Constantine the Great, 83, 102, 103
contado, 164, 165
conversion, 109–111
Copernicus, Nicolaus, 203
Copper Age, 24, 27–29, 37, 40–41
Corded Ware culture, 21, 30, 45, 80
Corpus Iuris Civilis, 134
Cose fiorentine (Francesco Guicciardini), 187
Council of Constance, 140–141
Counter-Reformation, 199–200
Courtier, The (Baldassare Castiglione), 177–178

Crusades, 131, 138, 140, 146,
149, 151
Curia Romana, 140, 146

D

Dante, 178
Dark Ages, 50, 69
Decameron (Giovanni
Boccaccio), 178
*Decline and Fall of the Roman Empire,
The* (Edward Gibbon), 96
Decretum, 134
devotio moderna, 199
dictatores, 172, 174
Dicuil the geographer, 117
Diocletian, 83
Dionysius Exiguus, 101
*Discourses on the First Ten Books of
Livy* (Niccolò Machiavelli),
183, 186
Divine Comedy, The (Dante), 178
domesticated animals, 13–19
Dominic of Guzmán, 144
Donatism, 106
Don Quixote (Miguel de
Cervantes), 201
Dorians, 69
Duby, Georges, 99

E

ecclesiastical discipline,
147–149
ecclesiastical organization,
137–143
ecclesiastical reform, 129–152
Ecerinis (Alberto Mussato), 172
Eckhart, Meister, 198

economy
Metal Ages, 36–62
Middle Ages, 125–126, 159
Neolithic Period, 13–18
Paleolithic Period, 3–4, 6
Renaissance, 188–195
education, 133–137, 176–177, 199
Eneolithic Period, 27
Enlightenment's view toward
Middle Ages, 95–97
Epipaleolithic Period, 10
Episcopal powers, 141
Erasmus, 94, 197, 199
Essay on Universal History, An
(Voltaire), 96
Estates-General, 156, 190
Este family, 180
ethnography, Roman, 103
Euric, 86

F

famine, 159
Ferdinand I, 193
Ferdinand II of Aragon, 191
feudalism, 124, 167
Fieschi, Sinibaldo, 132, 137
Flacius Illyricus, Matthias, 94
fossils, Paleolithic Period, 2–4
Francis of Assisi, 144
Franks, 82, 83, 85, 86, 92, 110,
115–122
Frederick I Barbarossa, 132
Frederick II, 132
Frederick III, 133
freedmen, 102
Friends of God, 198
Froissart, Jean, 200
Fust, Johann, 205

G

Galileo Galilei, 203
gender, burial practices and, 29, 45–46
Germans, 81–85, 103
German Theology, 198
Ghibellinism, 166
Gibbon, Edward, 96
Giotto, 94
Gli Asolani (Pietro Bembo), 178
Glossarium ad scriptores mediae et infimae latinitatis (Charles du Fresne), 95
Gnosticism, 106
Goldast, Melchior, 95
Golden Bull, 133
Goths, 82, 83, 87
government
  Greek, 69–70, 72
  Metal Ages, 47
  Middle Ages, 125–126
  Renaissance, 164–170
  Roman, 75–80
Gower, John, 200
grands rhetoriqueurs, 200
Gratian, Master, 134
Great Commission, the, 109–111
Great Interregnum, 133
Great Schism, 140
Greek Orthodox Church, 105
Greeks, 68–74
Gregorian reformers, 134
Gregory I (pope), 104
Gregory VII (pope), 130, 132, 139
Groote, Gerhard, 199
Grosseteste, Robert, 148
Guarino Veronese, 176
Guelfism, 166
Guicciardini, Francesco, 186–188
Gutenberg, Johannes, 205

H

Habsburg dynasty, 133, 189, 191, 195, 201
Hallstatt A-D, 26, 36, 39, 43–44, 52–53, 61
Harvey, William, 203
Haskins, Charles Homer, 98
Hellenes, 69
Henry III, 130
Henry IV (emperor), 132
Henry VI, 132
Henry VIII, 193
Henry of Segusio (Hostiensis), 137
heresy, 106, 148–149
Historiarum Florentini populi libri XII (Leonardo Bruni), 183
History of France (Jules Michelet), 163
History of Italy (Francesco Guicciardini), 187–188
Hohenstaufen dynasty, 132–133
Holy Roman Empire, 101–114, 129–133, 151
Honorius III, 140
Horn, Georg, 95
Hostiensis, 137
Hugh of Saint-Victor, 134
Huizinga, Johan, 159
humanism, 170–171, 180–188, 195–198
humanities, 177–180
Hundred Years' War, 190

Hungarian invasion, 121–122
Huns, 81–85

I

Ignatius of Loyola, 199–200
Imitation of Christ, The (Thomas
à Kempis), 199
Indo-Europeans, 22–23, 74–75
Innocent III (pope), 138, 144,
146, 149
Innocent IV (pope), 132, 137
inquisition, 149
Inquisition, Spanish, 149
Investiture Controversy, 132, 139, 152
Ionians, 69
Iron Age, 24, 31, 33, 35–36, 40,
42, 44, 45, 50, 55
burial practices during, 52–54
chronology of, 26
Germanic people during, 80
Isabella of Castile, 191
Islam, 114, 122, 131, 138–139,
149–151, 191
Italia mia (Petrarch), 178
Italian Renaissance, 163–188
culture during, 177–180
humanism during, 170–171,
180–188
humanities during, 173–176
language during, 173
literacy during, 172–173
philosophy during, 180–188
scholarship during, 176–177
urban growth during, 164–167
wars of expansion during,
168–170
Ivan III, 193
Ivo of Chartres, 134

J

Jerome, Father, 92
Jesuits, 199–200
Joachim of Fiore, 92
John of England, 138
John of the Cross, 200
Judaism, 108, 114, 139, 149–151, 191
Judaizing Christianity, 106
Julian, 83
Justinian, 87
Jutes, 85

K

Keller, Christoph, 95
Kempis, Thomas, 199
Kepler, Johannes, 203
Kuhn, Thomas, 203

L

Langland, William, 200
language, 22–23, 87, 173, 196
La Tène A-D, 26, 31, 39, 53–54, 61
Lateran Councils, 132, 139, 143,
146, 147, 150
LBK culture, 16–17
Leo III (pope), 119–120
Leo IX (pope), 130
Leonardo da Vinci, 204
Liber Censuum, 140
Life of Saint Antony
(Athanasius), 105
literacy, 172–173, 200–201
*Little Book of Eternal Wisdom,
The* (Heinrich Suso), 198
Little Book of Truth, The
(Heinrich Suso), 198

Lombard, Peter, 134–135
Lombards, 87, 119, 121, 132
Lothar of Segni, 146
Louis I (the Pious), 120
Luther, Martin, 94, 197, 199, 201

M

Macedonia, 80
Machiavelli, Niccolò, 178,
    182–188
Marcomanni, 82
Marcus Aurelius, 82, 101
Marlowe, Christopher, 201
marriage, 86, 157, 191–192
Martin, Alfred von, 169
Martin V (pope), 141
Martin of Braga, 105
Martin of Tours, 105, 109, 117
Medici, Cosimo de', 170
Medici, Lorenzo de', 179
Medici, de', family, 176, 185, 187
mendicant orders, 144
Merovingian dynasty, 115–117
Mesolithic Period, 8–12
Metal Ages, 15–16, 24–67
    burial practices during, 24, 25,
        40–46
    chronology of, 25–27
    control of natural resources
        during, 37–41
    culture during, 24, 43–44, 55–67
    economy during, 36–62
    migration during, 24
    mining techniques during, 37
    people of, 62–67
    political life during, 47
    religion during, 55–56
    social life/status during, 36–62

technology during, 37–39
trade during, 25, 26, 43, 52
urban growth during, 49–51
Michelet, Jules, 97, 163
Middle Ages, 89–161
    agricultural growth during,
        123–126
    chronology of, 100–101
    clergy during, 104–105
    coloni during, 102
    demographic growth during,
        123–126
    devotional life during,
        143–147
    ecclesiastical discipline during,
        147–149
    ecclesiastical organization
        during, 137–143
    Enlightenment's view toward,
        95–97
    Franks during, 115–122
    freedmen during, 102
    Holy Roman Empire during,
        101–114
    modern views of, 97–100
    monarchy during, 108–109,
        152–158
    origin of term, 91–101
    reform during, 129–152
    religion during, 101–151
    Romantic era's view toward,
        96–97
    slavery during, 102, 123–124
    social orders during,
        156–158
    technological innovation
        during, 126–127
    urban growth during,
        127–129

migration
    Barbarian, 80–88
    Greek, 69
    Indo-European, 22–23
    Mesolithic Period, 10
    Metal Ages, 24
    Neolithic Period, 13–15
    Roman, 74–75
Millaran culture, 28, 40
mining techniques, 37
missionaries, 109–111, 160–161
molds, use of, 31
monarchy, 108–109, 152–158,
    188–195
monasticism, 104–105, 143–144
Mongol invasions, 159
Montelius I-VI, 25, 43–44
Monumenta Germaniae
    Historica, 98
Mussato, Albertino, 172, 177
Mycenaean civilization, 69
mysticism, 198–200

N

Napoleon Bonaparte, 120, 133
natural resources, control of
    during Metal Ages, 37–41
nature, culture and, 55–56
Neolithic Period, 13–23, 25, 29,
    30, 45, 56
    agriculture during, 13–20
    building/settlement during,
        15, 16, 20–21
    burial practices during, 15, 16,
        21–22
    climate during, 20
    culture during, 13, 15–17, 20–22, 49
    domesticated animals during,
        13–19

economy during, 13–18
    migration during, 13–15
    population during, 20, 49
    religion during, 15, 16, 20–22
    settlement during, 15
    technology during, 14, 19–20
    textiles during, 18–19
    trade during, 22
    warfare during, 15, 17
New Monarchs, the, 190, 193
Newton, Isaac, 203
nicolaitism, 148
Nordic Bronze Age, 30
Northern Renaissance,
    188–201
    culture during, 200–201
    economy during, 188–195
    humanism during, 195–197
    literacy during, 200–201
    political life during,
        188–195
    religion during, 198–200
    social life/status during,
        188–195
*Nucleus of Middle History
    Between Ancient and
    Modern, The* (Christoph
    Keller), 95

O

Odoacer, 85
Oration on the Dignity of Man
    (Giovanni Pico della
    Mirandola), 182, 185
Order of Preachers, 144
Orlando furioso (Ludovico
    Ariosto), 178, 180
Orlando innamorato (Matteo
    Boiardo), 180

Orosius, Paulus, 92
Ostrogoths, 86
Otto I, 92, 121
Ottoman Empire, 151

P

Paleolithic Period, 1–8
papacy, 104, 111–114, 119–120, 129–152
parlamento, 165
Parliament, 155–156
Parthian Empire, 76
Patrick (patron saint of Ireland), 110
Paul the Apostle, 109
Paul the Deacon, 119
pax romana, 77
Pelagianism, 106
Penitentiary, 140
Peter of Piza, 119
Petrarch (Francesco Petrarca), 93–94, 173–175, 177–179, 181–182
Philip II of Spain, 191
philosophy, 180–188
Pippin, 119
Pippin II, 115
plague, 159
Pleistocene Epoch, 1–23
Politian (Angelo Poliziano), 176, 177
political life
    Greek, 69–70, 72
    Metal Ages, 47
    Middle Ages, 125–126, 152–158
    Renaissance, 164–170, 188–195
    Roman, 75–80
Pontano, Giovanni, 176, 177
population

Indo-European, 22–23
Middle Ages, 123–126
Neolithic Period, 20, 49
Paleolithic Period, 3, 5
prehistory, 1–23
Prince, The (Niccolò Machiavelli), 182, 183
principalities, 152–158
Ptolemy, 203

Q

Quintilian, 174

R

Rabelais, François, 201
Reformation, 129–152, 198
Reinecke, Paul, 25–26
religion
    Bronze Age, 55–62
    devotional life, 143–147
    ecclesiastical discipline, 147–149
    ecclesiastical organization, 137–143
    the Great Commission and, 109–111
    Greek, 70
    Holy Roman Empire, 101–114
    Metal Ages, 55–56
    Middle Ages, 101–151
    Neolithic Period, 15, 16, 20–22
    organization of imperial Christianity, 103–108
    Paleolithic Period, 6–8
    papacy and, 111–114
    Reformation, 129–152, 198
    Renaissance, 198–200
    Roman, 78–80
Remigius of Reims, 110

Renaissance, 162–208
  Carolingian, 171
  culture during, 177–180,
    200–201
  economy during, 188–195
  education during, 199
  humanism during, 170–171,
    180–188, 195–197
  humanities during, 173–176
  Italian, 163–188
  language during, 173
  literacy during, 172–173,
    200–201
  military during, 168–170
  monarchy during, 188–195
  Northern, 188–201
  philosophy during, 180–188
  political life during, 164–170,
    188–195
  religion during, 198–200
  scholarship during,
    176–177
  science during, 202–205
  social life/status during,
    188–195
  technology during, 202–205
  urban growth during, 164–167
  warfare during, 167–170,
    188–192, 204
*Renaissance of the Twelfth Century,
  The* (Charles Homer
  Haskins), 98
Renfrew, Colin, 45
Reuchlin, Johannes, 196
Rinaldi, Oderico, 94
Roman Curia, 140, 146
Roman de la rose, 200
Roman Rota, 140
Romans/Roman Empire, 74–80,
  86–88, 92
  Barbarians and, 80–88
  citizenry under, 77
  culture of, 86
  ethnography of, 103
  government of, 75–80
  impact of on future kingdoms,
    108, 156
  marriage and, 86
  migration and, 74–75
  organization of imperial
    Christianity, 103–108
  papacy and, 111–114
  political life of, 75–80
  reconfiguration of, 101–114
  religion and, 78–80, 101–114
Romantic era's view toward
  Middle Ages, 96–97
Rudolf I, 133

S

Salians, 121
Salutati, Coluccio, 183
salvation history, 92–93
Sannazzaro, Jacopo, 176
Sarton, George, 204
Saul of Tarsus (Paul the
  Apostle), 109
Savelli, Cencio, 140
Savonarola, Girolamo, 185, 189
Saxons, 82, 85, 88, 120–121
Scandinavian invasion, 121–122
Schöffer, Peter, 205
scholarship, 133–137, 176–177
science, 136–137, 202–205
Scythians, 54
Secretum meum (Petrarch), 182
Selden, John, 95
Sententiarum libri iv (Peter
  Lombard), 134–135

serfdom, 124, 167
settlement
  Bronze Age, 33–35
  Copper Age, 28
  Iron Age, 36
  Mesolithic Period, 12
  Middle Ages, 127–128
  Neolithic Period, 15, 16, 20–21
  Paleolithic Period, 5
Shakespeare, William, 201
sheet-metal working, 31
Ship of Fools, The (Sebastian
  Brant), 201
signoria, 167
simony, 148
Six Books of the Commonweal (Jean
  Bodin), 191
slavery, 77, 102, 123–124
Slavs, 88
social life/status
  Copper Age, 28
  Iron Age, 36
  Mesolithic Period, 12
  Metal Ages, 36–62
  Middle Ages, 156–158
  Neolithic Period, 20–22
  Renaissance, 188–195
  three orders of, 156–158
Society of Jesus, 199–200
Spiritual Exercises (Ignatius of
  Loyola), 199–200
studia humanitatis, 174
Suso, Heinrich, 198
Sutri, Synod of, 130
Swabian tribes, 81

T

Tartaglia, Niccolò, 204
Tasso, Torquato, 178

Tauler, Johann, 198
technology
  Bronze Age, 30, 33
  Mesolithic Period, 11–12
  Metal Ages, 37–39
  Middle Ages, 125–127
  Neolithic Period, 14, 19–20
  Paleolithic Period, 2, 5
  Renaissance, 202–205
Teresa of Avila, 200
territorial principalities,
  152–158
Teutoni, 81
textiles, 18–19
Theodore of Tarsus, 111
Theodoric the Ostrogoth, 86
Theodosius I, 103
Theodulf of Orleans, 119
Thomsen, Christian
  Jürgensen, 25
Three Age system, 25
three orders of society,
  156–158
trade
  Bronze Age, 25, 26, 30
  Iron Age, 36
  Mesolithic Period, 12
  Metal Ages, 25, 26, 43, 52
  Neolithic Period, 22
treaties, 83–85, 151
Trinitarianism, 106
Tumulus culture, 25, 42

U

Ulfilas, 87
Unetician culture, 25, 42,
  45–46
Upper Paleolithic Period, 1,
  4–8

Urban II, 130, 131, 140
urban growth
Metal Ages, 49–51
Middle Ages, 127–129
Renaissance, 164–167
Urnfield culture, 25–27, 31, 43, 45,
52, 60, 62

V

Valentinian I, 83
Valla, Lorenzo, 196
Valois kings, 189, 190
Vandals, 85
Vergerio, Pier Paolo, 174
vernacular literature, 176–180,
200–201
Vikings, 121–122
Villon, François, 201
Vincent of Lérins, 106
Visconti, Gian Galeazzo, 170
Visconti family, 183
Visigoths, 85, 86, 110, 115, 117

Vittorino da Feltre, 176
Voetius, Gisbertus, 95
Voltaire, 96

W

warfare/military
Bronze Age, 33–36
Copper Age, 28
Iron Age, 35–36
Middle Ages, 125–126, 131, 138,
140, 146, 149, 151, 160
Neolithic Period, 15, 17
Renaissance, 167–170, 188–
192, 204
waterways, 28, 126–127
Whitby, Synod of, 110–111
Windesheim Congregation, 199
Worms, Concordat of, 139

Z

Zabarella, Jacopo, 203